A
DICTIONARY
OF
EMINENT LIBRARIANS

A DICTIONARY OF EMINENT LIBRARIANS

ROBERT B. DOWNS

HIGH PLAINS PUBLISHING COMPANY, INC.
WORLAND, WYOMING

ISBN: 0-962333-5-2
LIBRARY OF CONGRESS NUMBER : 90-84054

Printed in the United States of America

FIRST EDITION
1 2 3 4 5 6 7 8 9

Design and Typography by:
SHADOW CANYON GRAPHICS
Evergreen, Colorado

HIGH PLAINS PUBLISHING COMPANY
Post Office Box 1860
Worland, Wyoming 82401

Contents

PREFACE

This work identifies the many men and women who have contributed substantially toward shaping the modern library world, playing leading roles in various types of activity that in one way or another make twentieth-century college, university, public, school, and special libraries distinctive from those of the past.

The individuals whose lives are sketched in the following accounts were leaders introducing changes in library administration, library architecture, library cooperation, collection development, national bibliography and bibliographic control, library education, automation, and intellectual freedom — changes that have made librarianship a true profession.

While the list is international, most of the names are of librarians from the United States, Britain, and Western Europe. Most of them served their profession after 1800, when the vocation began to be well-defined.

No attempt has been made to classify the librarians by type; too many have moved from one area to another during their careers.

Robert B. Downs
Urbana, Illinois
July 1990

Acknowledgments

Patricia Stenstrom, who tracked down key information, and other colleagues on the University of Illinois Library staff deserve to be remembered for providing me with valuable assistance in selecting the librarians to be included in this book. Jane B. Downs offered encouragement and general assistance.

Every teacher learns from his students. I am no exception, and I am especially indebted to and take particular pride in the significant contributions that have been made by, among others, Furuzan Olşen, director of the Middle East Technical University Library in Ankara, Turkey; Rhoda Barry in South Africa; Sister Francis Dolores Donnelly in Canada; Naomi Fukuda in Japan; Takeo Urata, director of the Tokyo University Library; Ursula Picache of the Institute of Library Science in the Philippines; Mohammed El Hadi of Egypt; Madoko Kon and Yuni Monji of Japan; and Osman Ersoy, director of the Turkish Library School in Ankara.

For preparation of the manuscript, I am deeply indebted to Deloris Holiman, Kim Trumbull, Sheryl Gocking, and Sonya Kruse. To Clara Downs Keller I owe special thanks for the construction of an excellent index.

EMINENT LIBRARIANS

ACKERMAN, PAGE (1912-) was born in Evanston, Illinois,
graduated from Agnes Scott College in 1933, and received a B.S.
in library science from the University of North Carolina in 1940.
She was a school librarian in the Druid Hills School of Emory
University, 1939-1940, cataloger in the Columbia Theological
Seminary at Decatur, Georgia, 1942-1943, post librarian at the
U.S. Army Aberdeen Proving Ground, 1945, assistant librarian of
the Union Theological Seminary at Richmond, Virginia, 1945-
1949, reference librarian at the University of California in Los
Angeles, 1949-1954, assistant librarian, 1954-1965, and associate
librarian, 1965-1973, of UCLA . She was appointed UCLA librarian in 1973 and remained in that position until 1977.

After her retirement from UCLA, Miss Ackerman began teaching
at the School of Library and Information Studies at Berkeley,
California.

ADAMS, RANDOLPH GREENFIELD (1892-1951) was born in
Philadelphia and graduated from the University of Pennsylvania.
He won a Ph.D. degree from the University of Pennsylvania in
1920. From 1917 to 1919, he served in the U.S. Army. From

1920 to 1923, he was professor of history at Duke University. In 1923, he was appointed director of the William L. Clements Library at the University of Michigan and held that post until his death in 1951. Under Adams's leadership, the Clements Library became recognized as one of the nation's great repositories of American history.

Adams, Scott (1909-1982) was born in Agawam, Massachusetts, and graduated from Yale in 1930 and from the Columbia Library School in 1940. In between, he served as an ordinary seaman on voyages to South America and was a wholesale book salesman. He progressed from a job in the order department at Teachers College Library to head the order and catalog departments of the Providence, Rhode Island, Public Library. He later became chief of the Army Medical Library Acquisition Division. He joined the Library of Congress mission to Europe in 1946 to acquire wartime publications. After his return to Washington, Adams served as acting director of the Army Medical Library from 1946 to 1950. In 1950, he became librarian of the National Institutes of Health (NIH) in Bethesda, Maryland. In 1959, he left NIH to become director of the foreign science information program of the National Science Foundation. In 1960, he returned to his old institution to become deputy director of the National Library of Medicine. International activities included missions in Korea, Vietnam, Egypt, and Soviet Russia.

Adams was active in several professional organizations: he was president of the District of Columbia Library Association, 1947-1948; president of the American Documentation Institute, 1954-1955; and president of the Medical Library Association, 1967-1968.

Ahern, Mary Eileen (1860-1938) was born on a farm near Indianapolis, Indiana, and graduated from Central Normal College, Danville, Indiana, in 1881. She attended the Armour Institute of Technology Library School in Chicago from 1895 to 1896. Her library career began in 1889 with an appointment as assistant state librarian of Indiana, a position that she held until 1893. From 1893 to 1895, she served as state librarian. She was instrumental in establishing the Indiana Library Association in 1889 and served as its president in 1895.

While a student at Armour Institute, Miss Ahern was appointed editor of a new journal, *Public Libraries*, designed to help small public libraries. She remained as its editor during the entire life of the journal, from 1896 to 1931, with a total of thirty-six volumes, until it ceased publication. It became the official organ of the Illinois Library Association. Mary Ahern served three terms as president of the Illinois Library Association, in 1908, 1909, and 1915. In 1897, she attended the Second International Library Conference in England.

AKERS, SUSAN GREY (1889-1984) was born in Richmond, Kentucky, graduated from the University of Kentucky in 1909, and received a certificate from the University of Wisconsin Library School in 1913. A Ph.D. from the Graduate Library School of the University of Chicago followed in 1933.

Miss Akers's library career started in 1911 when she became a general assistant in the Louisville Public Library. From 1913 to 1920, she was on the Wellesley College Library staff. From 1920 to 1922, she was head of the catalog department of the North Dakota State Library, and from 1922 to 1928 she was a faculty member of the University of Wisconsin Library School. She went to the University of North Carolina Library School in 1931 and rose to deanship of the school from 1935 until her retirement in 1954. She had assignments in Tokyo, 1950-1951, and at the University of Tehran, 1954-1955.

From 1943 to 1946, Miss Akers was president of the North Carolina Library Association. She was the author of *Simple Library Cataloging* (1927), which, with periodical revisions, has remained the basic text in its field. She was given the Margaret Mann award in 1956.

ANDERSON, EDWIN HATFIELD (1861-1947), one of the great names in American library history, was born in Zionsville, Indiana. He graduated from Wabash College in 1883 and from the New York State Library School at Albany, directed by Melvil Dewey. Anderson started work as a cataloger at the new Newberry Library in 1891. He left Chicago in 1892 to become librarian of the Carnegie Free Library in Braddock, Pennsylvania. A greater opportunity came his way in 1895, when he was appointed to head the Carnegie Library of Pittsburgh. Under his leadership, the library was transformed into an institution boasting an excellent staff, a strong collection, a printed book catalog, a department of technology, children's services in the central building and branches, and a training school — the forerunner of the Carnegie Library School. In 1901-1902, he was president of the Keystone State Library Association.

Anderson resigned from Pittsburgh in 1904, and after an interim went on to succeed Melvil Dewey as director of the New York State Library and the New York State Library School. While there, he planned a new building, strengthened library extension work, and added new faculty members for the school. In 1907-1908, he also served as president of the New York Library Association.

Anderson made another move in 1908, when he became assistant director of the New York Public Library. In 1913, he succeeded John Shaw Billings as director. He remained in this position for the next twenty-one years, during which the NYPL became the largest and most used public library in the world. There were two distinct divisions: the reference department — a great research library — occupying a new central library building; and a circulation department, with some forty-six branches. Under Anderson, a library for the blind, a municipal reference library, a manuscript division, a music library, a picture and theater collection, and the Schomburg collection of Negro history and literature were established. A readers' advisory service was started under Jennie M. Flexner, and children's work under Anne Carroll Moore became nationally famous. The New York Public Library School opened in 1911, with Mary Wright Plummer as principal. It later merged with the New York State Library School at Columbia Univesity.

Anderson was president of the American Library Association in 1913-1914, and he also headed other library organizations, such as the New York Library Association and the New York Literary Club.

ANDREWS, CLEMENT WALKER (1858-1930), the organizer and first librarian of the John Crerar Library, was a graduate of the Boston Latin School and Harvard University. Through graduate work in chemistry and serving as librarian of the Massachusetts Institute of Technology, he became familiar with chemical literature and other fields of the pure and applied sciences. His linguistic knowledge of classical and modern languages was also extensive. Under Andrews's direction, The Crerar Library adopted a classed, rather than a dictionary catalog and produced printed catalog cards for distribution to other libraries. Andrews participated directly in the development of the Crerar's collections, carried on correspondence with book dealers, and spent hours checking trade publications and bibliographies for desired material.

Andrews was an active member of the library profession and served as president of the American Library Association in 1906-1907.

ASH, LEE (1917-) was born in New York City and holds library science degrees from Pratt and Chicago. He is one of the most active surveyors of libraries, including Harvard Medical Library, Boston Medical Library, Toronto Public Library, University of Rochester, Queens Borough Public Library, and others. His career has also encompassed editorial activities: he has served as editor of the *Library Journal*, 1957-1959; as editor of *American Notes and Queries*, starting in 1962; as editor of several editions of *Who's Who in Library Service*; and as author of *Guide to Subject Collections in Libraries*. He has participated actively in professional library organizations and has served as president of the New York Library Club.

ASHEIM, LESTER EUGENE (1914-) was born in Spokane, Washington, and graduated from the University of Washington with both bachelor's and master's degrees. In 1949, he received a Ph.D. from the University of Chicago. He was a reference assistant at the University of Washington, 1937-1941, librarian of the U.S. Federal Penitentiary on McNeil Island, 1941-1942, and in the U.S. Army, 1942-1945. He joined the University of Chicago Graduate Library School faculty in 1948 and served as dean of the school from 1952 to 1961. From 1961 to 1966, Asheim was director of the American Library Association's (ALA) International Relations Office, and he traveled widely, especially in newly developing nations. He returned to his primary field as director of ALA's Office for Library Education in 1966. From 1971 to 1974, he returned to the Graduate Library School faculty. In 1974, he became a member of the faculty of the University of North Carolina Library School. He retired in 1984.

Asheim is the author of a number of significant books on library education, mass communications, international librarianship and library manpower. He received the Beta Phi Mu Award for distinguished service to education for librarianship in 1973, was elected president of the ALA Library Education Division in 1976, and was awarded an honorary life member of the ALA in 1984.

ASKEW, SARAH BYRD (1863-1942) was born in Alabama and graduated from high school, but she never went to college. However, she attended Pratt Institute to study library work. Her first library experience was a temporary appointment in a branch of the Cleveland Public Library. After finishing at Pratt, she was appointed to organize the New Jersey Library Commission. Under Askew, the library movement in New Jersey began to gain momentum, aided by key groups that she inspired and recruited. During World War I, she was head of the New Jersey Library War Service to distribute books to camps, stations, and hospitals, and during World War II, she helped to organize the Victory Book Campaign. New Jersey, stimulated by Miss Askew, became recognized nationally as one of the pioneers in the county library movement. To encourage professional library training, she conducted a summer school for librarians from 1906 until her death in 1942.

ATKINSON, HUGH CRAIG (1933-1986), a native of Chicago, was a graduate of the University of Chicago and began his library career as an assistant in special collections with the University of Chicago Library. Later work included positions with Pennsylvania Military College, the State University of New York at Buffalo, and Ohio State University, where he became director of libraries. The remainder of his professional career, 1976-1986, was spent as university librarian at the University of Illinois Library at Urbana-Champaign. At Illinois, he created the Illinois LCS network statewide for library cooperation, based on the use of library automation. A major addition to the main library building at Illinois under his supervision provided greatly increased capacity of the book stacks.

BABB, JAMES TINKHAM (1899-1968) was born in Lewiston, Idaho, and graduated from Yale University in 1924. From 1924 to 1926, he was a student at Yale Law School, and for the next twelve years he was an investment banker. Beginning in his under-graduate days, he became an active book collector, and in 1938, he gave up his business career to become assistant librarian of Yale University Library. Five years later, he was appointed university librarian. In that position, he was also in charge of Yale's twenty-eight school and departmental libraries, including those of law and medicine. Babb's emphasis as chief librarian was on the acquisition of a number of outstanding special collections. He was president of the Connecticut Library Association from 1945 to 1946, and past president of the Bibliographical Society of America.

Baker, Augusta Alexander (1911-   ) was born in Baltimore, Maryland, graduated from New York State College at Albany in 1933, and received an M.S. in library science in 1934. She served as a children's librarian in the New York Public Library from 1937 to 1961. She was a consultant for the Trinidad Public Library in 1953, an instructor at the Columbia School of Library Service, and a lecturer at the Rutgers Graduate Library School between 1956 and 1967. In 1967-1968, she was president of the ALA Children's Service Division. Her awards include the ALA Clarence Day Award and the Grolier Award, 1968; the *Parent's Magazine* Medal, 1966; and the Dutton-MacRae Award, 1953. Mrs. Baker is the author of a number of anthologies of children's stories and is joint author on several works on storytelling. In the thirteen years during which she was coordinator of children's services for the New York Public Library, she expanded the collection to include records and tapes and started weekly radio and television broadcasts. She was also active in the television program "Sesame Street." She conducted workshops and institutes on storytelling and materials for children in various states and Australia. She participated in the White House Conference on Children in 1970. She was also the recipient of honorary doctorates and won a distinguished service award from the State University of New York at Albany in 1974. She was elected an honorary member of the American Library Association in 1975.

Barker, Tommie Dora (1888-1978) was born in Rockmart, Georgia, attended Agnes Scott College in Atlanta from 1907 to 1909, and received a certificate from the Atlanta Carnegie Library School in 1909. Her career was devoted to the development and extension of library service in the Southeast. She began as an assistant in the Alabama Department of Archives and History Library Extension in 1909. From 1911 to 1930, she was on the staff of the Atlanta Public Library, first as a reference librarian and instructor in the Atlanta Library School, 1911-1915, and then as director of the school, 1915-1930. She encouraged transfer of the school to Emory University.

From 1930 to 1936, Miss Barker was the Southern regional field agent for the American Library Association to promote library service in the region. She was appointed dean of the Emory University Library School in 1936 and directed the school until her retirement in 1954.

Miss Barker was president of the Georgia Library Association, 1920-1921; of the Southeastern Library Association, 1926-1928; of the Association of American Library Schools, 1939-1940; and of the Atlanta Library Club, 1943-1944.

BASCOM, ELVIRA LUCILE (1870-1945) graduated from Allegheny College in 1894 and was on the New York State Library staff under Melvil Dewey from 1900 to 1908. She earned a B.S. in library science from the New York School of Librarians in 1901. From 1908 to 1913, she was employed by the Wisconsin Free Library Commission in Madison as a book selection expert, compiling the *ALA Booklist*. After World War I, she was in the Children's Bureau in Washington. From 1919 to 1925, she was head of the Library Science Department at the University of Texas. In 1929, she went on to Pittsburgh to join the faculty of the Carnegie Library School and retired in 1937 to live in Cleveland. Miss Bascom compiled the *ALA Catalog*, 1904-1911, and was author of a standard work, *Book Selection*, published by the ALA in 1925.

BAY, JENS CHRISTIAN (1871-1962) was born in Denmark and studied in Copenhagen. In 1892, he was employed by the Missouri Botanical Garden to catalog illustrations and review scientific literature. In 1901, he joined the Library of Congress staff to develop the classification scheme for medicine and other scientific fields.

Bay moved to Chicago in 1905 to succeed Clement Walker Andrews as director of the John Crerar Library. He was a productive scholar and great book collector. His collection on Western exploration went to the Missouri Historical Society in Columbia, and a second collection of 14,000 volumes, rich in Danish literature, was acquired by the University of Kentucky Library. Bay died at the age of ninety-one.

BEALS, RALPH ALBERT (1899-1954) was born in Deming, New Mexico, and graduated from the University of California at Berkeley in 1921. He received a master's degree in English from Harvard in 1925. He remained at Harvard until 1928 as an assistant in English and was an English instructor at New York University from 1928 to 1933. From 1933 to 1939, Beals was assistant to the director of the American Association for Adult Education. Influenced by Frederick Keppel, president of the Carnegie Corporation of New York, he entered the University of Chicago Graduate Library School as a candidate for the doctorate. He had previously received the certificate of the Riverside Library School and had served as camp librarian at one of the military installations in the Southwest.

After leaving Chicago, Beals was assistant director of the District of Columbia Public Library from 1940 to 1942. He returned to Chicago to accept the directorship of the University of Chicago Library from 1942 to 1946. During the last year of his tenure there, he also served as dean of the graduate library school.

In 1946, the board of trustees of the New York Public Library invited Beals to become the director of that institution. With some hesitation he accepted, though his early death prevented lengthy service in the position. He died at age fifty-five. The NYPL made major progress on a number of fronts during his administration. His influence extended also to the state of New York. He was president of the New York Library Association and was active in a number of literary and scholarly organizations.

BECKLEY, JOHN JAMES (1757-1807) was chosen in 1802 by his old friend, Thomas Jefferson, to be the first librarian of Congress. Beckley served at the same time as clerk of the House of

Representatives. Jefferson advised on the choice of books to be acquired by the library. By 1814, about three thousand volumes had accumulated. Then disaster struck. British forces captured Washington and burned the Capitol, using books from the library as kindling. Congress promptly appropriated funds to repair the damage and, if possible, to replace the books.

BEER, WILLIAM (1849-1927) was born in Plymouth, England. In 1867-1871, he was one of the directors of the Cottonian Library of Plymouth. He worked for a time in the Newcastle Public Library, where he took a special interest in developing an excellent collection on the literature of Northumberland. In 1884, Beer emigrated to Canada, but he soon settled in the United States. After a few years of practicing mining engineering, he became librarian of the Topeka (Kansas) Public Library in 1889. While there, he organized a series of extension lectures. Two years later, he was made librarian of the newly organized Howard Memorial Library of New Orleans. In 1896, he was also appointed librarian of the New Orleans Public Library. That position was resigned in 1906 in order for Beer to devote himself exclusively to the Howard Library, which became an important reference library giving particular attention to Louisiana history and literature. Beer was prominent in the social and literary life of New Orleans for many years, living to the age of seventy-eight.

BELDEN, CHARLES FRANCIS DORR (1870-1931) was born in Syracuse, New York, and graduated from Harvard in 1895. He received a law degree from Harvard in 1898. For three years, he served as secretary for the law faculty. In 1902, he was appointed assistant librarian of the law library. Over the next seven years, he completed a *Catalogue of the Library of the Law School of Harvard University*, published in two volumes in 1909. In 1908-1909, Belden directed the Boston Social Law Library, after which he was appointed state librarian of Massachusetts. During the eight years that he held that position, he was president of the Massachusetts Library Club, 1911-1913, and of the National Association of State Librarians, 1911-1912.

In 1917, Belden was elected librarian of the Boston Public Library. The resources of the library were increased substantially during his administration by the addition of several important special collections. Circulation also doubled, and the number of branch libraries was increased.

Belden was elected president of the American Library Association for the 1925-1926 term.

BEUST, NORA E. (1888-1973) was born in New Albany, Indiana, and graduated from the University of Wisconsin in 1929. She earned a certificate from the University of Wisconsin Library School in 1913, was a member of the Cleveland training classes in 1914, and earned a master's degree in education from the University of North Carolina in 1930. Her positions included branch librarian at the Chicago Public Library, 1912; reference librarian at Wisconsin State Teachers College at La Crosse, 1914-1916; first assistant and children's librarian at La Crosse, 1916-1918 and 1923-1927; librarian for the school of education, University of North Carolina, 1927-1929; and associate professor at the University of North Carolina Library School, 1930-1937. She was president of the North Carolina Library Association from 1935 to 1936. In 1937, she was appointed the first specialist in school and children's libraries in the U.S. Office of Education. She was a noted professor of children's literature and was especially interested and influential in encouraging and teaching storytelling. She was considered one of the top children's librarians in the country by Louis Round Wilson, who helped her secure the position with the U.S. Office of Education. She was active in the ALA and was central to organizations at the state and national levels for the promotion of children's library services.

BILLINGS, JOHN SHAW (1838-1913) was born in Indiana, graduated from Miami University at Oxford, Ohio, and received an M.D. from the Medical College of Ohio. Early in his career, Billings noted the need for a great medical library in the United States. His opportunity came when he was put in charge of the Surgeon-General's Library in Washington, D.C. He was responsible for printing the monumental, sixteen-volume *Index-Catalogue* to the Surgeon-General's Library. In 1879, publication was begun of the *Index Medicus*, a monthly guide to current medical literature. Recognition of Billings's contributions to medical science came in his election to the presidency of the American Public Health Association.

After his retirement from the army, Billings spent the next seventeen years consolidating the Astor, Lenox, and Tilden foundations to create the New York Public Library. The city gave land in a central location, and the library building constructed upon it followed the plan sketched by Billings. New York's numerous free circulating libraries became branches of the central library, aided by a five-million-dollar Carnegie grant.

During his last eleven years, Billings was active in the organization and guidance of the Carnegie Institution of Washington, established to promote scientific research.

BILLINGTON, JAMES HADLEY (1929-) holds degrees from Princeton and Oxford and was appointed librarian of Congress by President Reagan in 1987 to succeed Daniel Boorstin. He is a historian and has taught and lectured in the United States and in foreign countries, including the Soviet Union, Finland, France, and countries in Asia. His published works have focused particularly on Slavic studies.

BISHOP, DAVID FULTON (1937-) began his professional career as a technical services coordinator for the University of Chicago from 1969 to 1970. In 1973, he became head cataloger and held that position until 1975. He served as a technical services assistant at the University of Maryland from 1975 to 1979. He earned a master's degree in library science from the Catholic University of

America in 1964, and a B.M. degree from the Eastman School of Music in 1959. He served as director of libraries at the University of Georgia from 1979 until his appointment as university librarian at the University of Illinois in 1987. He has been a member of the Association of Research Libraries board of directors since 1986.

BISHOP, WILLIAM WARNER (1871-1955) was born in Hannibal, Missouri, and held bachelor's and master's degrees from the University of Michigan as well as numerous honorary degrees. Over a lengthy period, he was regarded as a giant among American university librarians. His first library-oriented position was at Garrett Biblical Institute in Evanston, Illinois, from 1895 to 1898, as an instructor in the New Testament and as an assistant librarian. This appointment was followed by positions as a librarian and instructor in Latin at the Polytechnic Institute of Brooklyn, 1899-1902; as head cataloger in the Princeton University Library, 1902-1904; as reference librarian at Princeton, 1904-1907; as superintendent of the reading room at the Library of Congress, 1907-1915; and finally as librarian of the University of Michigan, 1915-1941. In association activities, Bishop was president of the American Library Association from 1918 to 1919, president of the International Federation of Library Associations from 1931 to 1936, and president of the Bibliographical Society of America from 1921 to 1923. In 1927, Bishop headed a project for the recataloging and reorganization of the Vatican Library.

BLACKBURN, ROBERT HAROLD (1919-) was born in Vegreville, Canada, and graduated from the University of Alberta in 1941. He received a master's degree in English from the University of Toronto in 1942, and an M.S. in library science from Columbia University in 1947. During World War II, he was in the Royal Canadian Air Force. From 1945 to 1946, he was a general assistant in the Calgary Public Library, after which he became assistant librarian of the University of Toronto, 1947-1954. After 1954, he was promoted to chief librarian. He toured German libraries as a guest of the West German government in 1964.

Blackburn was president of the Canadian Library Association in 1958-1959 and president of the Canadian Association of College and University Libraries in 1963-1964.

BLISS, HENRY EVELYN (1870-1955) was born in New York City. His entire career was associated with the College of the City of New York (CCNY), where he served as head of departmental libraries beginning in 1925, and as associate librarian from 1928 until his retirement.

Bliss is remembered chiefly for the classification system that he devised for libraries, a plan that he hoped would rival the Dewey decimal and Library of Congress classifications. The scheme was adopted by CCNY but was never accepted by other American libraries. It met a more favorable reception abroad, where more than fifty libraries in Britain, Nigeria, Australia, and New Zealand adopted the scheme. Bliss's ideas were presented in a book published in 1929, *The Organizations of Knowledge and the System of the Sciences..*

BLUE, THOMAS FOUNTAIN (1866-1935) was born in Farmville, Virginia, the son of former slaves. He attended Hampton Institute and graduated from the Richmond Theological Seminary in 1898. He began his library career as a branch librarian in the Louisville Free Public Library in 1905. His duties were expanded until he was appointed head of the "colored department" of the Louisville Library in 1919. One of his major achievements was the establishment of the library apprenticeship training program for black library personnel, to which a number of large southern public libraries sent staff for professional training.

BOAZ, MARTHA (1913-) was born in Stuart, Virginia, and graduated from Madison College in 1935. She holds library science degrees from Peabody and the University of Michigan. Early positions included school librarian at Bridgewater, Virginia, 1935-

1937; school librarian at Jeffersontown, Kentucky, 1937-1940; assistant librarian at Madison College, 1940-1949; associate professor of library services at the University of Tennessee, 1950-1951; instructor at the University of Michigan Library School, 1951-1952; and staff member of the Pasadena, California, Public Library, 1952.

In 1953, Miss Boaz joined the faculty of the School of Library Science at the University of Southern California and remained there for twenty-five years. As dean for twenty-three years, she developed the school into one of the leading library schools in the United States. In 1974, the school occupied its own building on the USC campus.

Miss Boaz was president of the ALA Library Education Division, 1968-1969; president of the California Library Association, 1962; and president of the Association of American Library Schools, 1961-1962. She had missions abroad in Pakistan and Vietnam.

BODLEY, SIR THOMAS (1545-1613), born in Exeter and educated at Geneva, was in the English diplomatic service from 1585 to 1596. He retired from public service and devoted himself to reestablishing the Oxford University Library, which had been almost totally destroyed between 1550 and 1556 during the purge of libraries by Edward VI. Through Bodley's generosity and gifts from his friends, the library was opened formally in 1602 and named the Bodleian. It has the distinction of being the first public library in Europe and the second largest in England, after the British Museum. A theologian, Thomas James, was appointed librarian in residence and remained in that post until 1620 at an annual salary of forty pounds. By the end of its first century, the Bodleian held 25,000 volumes and 7,000 manuscripts.

BOGLE, SARAH COMLY NORRIS (1870-1932) was a native of Milton, Pennsylvania, and spent a year as a student at the University of Chicago. She graduated from the Drexel Institute Library School in Philadelphia in 1904. She spent three years as librarian of Juniata College in Huntingdon, Pennsylvania, and had a brief stay at the Queens Borough (New York) Public Library. She then went on to the Carnegie Library of Pittsburgh as branch librarian, and later as head of the children's department and principal of the library school for children's librarians. She was president of the Association of American Library Schools from 1917 to 1918.

In 1920, Miss Bogle became assistant secretary of the American Library Association, where she remained associated with Carl H. Milam, the executive secretary, for the rest of her career. In that position she served also as secretary of the ALA Board of Education for Librarianship, 1924-1932, and as director of the Paris Library School, 1924-1929, during its short life.

BOLTON, CHARLES KNOWLES (1867-1950) was born in Cleveland, Ohio, and graduated from Harvard in 1890. From 1890 to 1893, he was an assistant in the Harvard University Library and then became librarian of the Brookline Public Library in suburban Boston. On the basis of his demonstrated administrative abilities, in 1898 he was appointed librarian of the Boston Athenaeum, a position that he held for thirty-five years, until 1933. From 1907 to 1920, he also served on the faculty of Simmons College Library School. He was dedicated to research and writing and produced a number of books on the history of colonial New England, genealogy, and heralding. His *Bolton's American Armory* is still a standard work.

BOMAR, CORA PAUL (1913-) was born in Memphis, Tennessee, and graduated from the University of Tennessee in 1939. She received a B.S. in library science from Peabody in 1946 and a master's degree in education from the University of North Carolina in 1950. After varied experience as a high school and junior college librarian from 1941 to 1951, she became head supervisor in the library and instructional materials service section of the North Carolina Department of Public Instruction from 1951 to 1969. She was president of the American Association of School

Librarians from 1962 to 1963, president of the ALA Library Education Division from 1969 to 1970, president of the Southeastern Library Association from 1968 to 1969, and international president of the library honorary society, Beta Phi Mu.

From 1969 to 1979, when she retired, Miss Bomar was on the faculty of the University of North Carolina Library School at Greensboro, where she assisted in the development of the master of library science degree. She returned after retirement to assist in accreditation for the library school. Perhaps her greatest influence and contribution to the profession came with her role in creating and explaining the program for funding of libraries under President Lyndon Johnson.

BONTEMPS, ARNA WENDELL (1902-1973) was born in Alexandria, Louisiana. After his family moved to California, he graduated from Pacific Union College in 1923, and some years later, in 1943, he received a master's degree from the Graduate Library School of the University of Chicago. Rosenwald fellowships for creative writing were awarded him in 1929 and 1954. He became recognized as one of America's pioneer black authors and librarians. After a career as a writer, Bontemps became librarian of Fisk University in Nashville, Tennessee, succeeding Louis Shores and Carl White. One of his achievements at Fisk was the extensive development of the Negro collection. After his retirement in 1964, Bontemps taught at the University of Illinois in Chicago and at Yale University. His literary efforts were rewarded with a number of important awards.

BOORSTIN, DANIEL J. (1914-), appointed by President Gerald R. Ford, was librarian of Congress from 1975 until 1987. In 1978, under his direction, there was a major reorganization of the Library of Congress, the first in thirty-five years. Seven departments of the library were established: management, national programs, research services, processing services, copyright office, law library, and congressional research service. Boorstin is a leading American historian, the author of numerous works, and a graduate of Harvard, Oxford, and Yale. He has taught and lectured in many universities and colleges, both foreign and domestic.

BORGES, JORGE LUIS (1899-), a native of Buenos Aires, is best known as Argentina's leading poet, short story writer, essayist, and critic. He was professor of literature at the University of Argentina, and, in 1955, after the fall of Juan Perón, he was named director of the National Library of Argentina. His library career had begun earlier as an assistant in a small municipal library in Buenos Aires. He had been fired from that job for opposing the Perón dictatorship. Borges has made several lecture tours of the United States and has served as a visiting professor at the University of Texas and Harvard University.

BOSTWICK, ARTHUR E. (1860-1942) was a native of Litchfield, Connecticut. He graduated from Yale University, including receiving a Ph.D. in physical science. After several editorial positions, Bostwick was appointed librarian of the Free Circulating Library of New York. As a librarian, he wrote a standard work on the *American Public Library*, edited the American Library Pioneers series, lectured to library schools, advised on library building plans, and made surveys of libraries, such as the Boston Public Library. The Free Circulating Library was amalgamated with the New York Public Library, and Bostwick became chief of the circulation department. In 1909, he became librarian of the St. Louis Public Library, and he served for thirty-two years as chief librarian, a period during which the library set up many more branches and greatly increased the size of its staff, its circulation, and the number of borrowers. In the international field, Bostwick went to China, Rome, and Venice as representative of the American Library Association. He was president of the ALA in 1907-1908.

BOUSFIELD, HUMPHREY G. (1903-) was born in Newark, New Jersey. He graduated from New York University in 1931 and received a B.S. in library science from Columbia in 1937. He was supervisor of evening services at New York University, 1927-1929; chief of the readers department, Washington Square Library of New York University, 1929-1931; assistant director of the University of Illinois Library at Urbana, 1943-1944; and chief librarian of Brooklyn College, 1944-1972. Bousfield is co-author with Charles H. Brown of a standard work, *Circulation Work in College and University Libraries* (1933).

BOWERMAN, GEORGE FRANKLIN (1868-1940) was born in Farmington, New York, and graduated from the University of Rochester in 1892. He met Melvil Dewey at the Chicago World's Fair in 1893; Dewey approved his employment as a reference librarian at the New York State Library while Bowerman was earning a B.L.S. degree from the New York State Library School in 1895. A year was spent as a reference librarian at the Reynolds Library in Rochester, after which Bowerman returned to the New York State Library from 1897 to 1898. The next move was to New York City, where Bowerman worked for the *New York Tribune* and the *New International Encyclopedia* from 1898 to 1900. Returning to the library field, Bowerman became director of the Wilmington (Delaware) Institute Free Library from 1901 to 1904.

In 1904 came the appointment that was to round out the rest of Bowerman's career, when he was named head of the District of Columbia Library. He directed a phenomenal growth of a small, weak institution into a major public library, with twelve branches, service to 180 schools, hospitals, and government agencies, a strong staff, and adequate budget. He retired at age seventy-two.

Bowerman was president of the District of Columbia Library Association from 1906 to 1907 and vice-president of the International Congress of Librarians in Brussels in 1910. He was treasurer of the American Library Association in 1906. He was an avid traveler to Alaska, Central America, Mexico, Russia, and frequently to Europe.

BOWKER, RICHARD ROGERS (1848-1933), a native of Salem, Massachusetts, graduated from the College of the City of New York in 1868. He was highly versatile: he was an editor, publisher, bibliographer, author, and library promoter. He became city editor of the newly established *New York Evening Mail* and, a year later, in 1869, the paper's literary editor. In 1875, he joined the literary department of the *New York Tribune*. From 1873, Bowker was a regular contributor to Frederick Leypoldt's *Publishers' Weekly*. In 1879, he bought *Publishers' Weekly* and began publishing the *American Catalogue*, listing all books in print in the United States. He was editor of *Publishers' Weekly* for the rest of his life and edited the *American Catalogue* through 1910.

In cooperation with Leypoldt and Melvil Dewey, Bowker founded the *Library Journal* and, a month later, took part in the organizational meeting of the American Library Association in Philadelphia in 1876. In recognition of his efforts, the ALA elected him honorary president for its fiftieth anniversary year. Bowker was the first president of the New York Library Club (1885) and a trustee of the Brooklyn Library from 1888 until his death.

In a conference with President William McKinley, Bowker influenced the president to appoint Herbert Putnam as librarian of Congress.

BOYD, ANNE MORRIS (1884-1974) was born in Arcola, Illinois. She was a student from 1900 to 1901 at the University of Kentucky and graduated later, in 1906, from Milliken University. Her first library job was as an assistant in the Decatur (Illinois) Public Library. After completing college, she became librarian, in 1906, of the Kansas State Agricultural College. She spent 1908-1909 with the St. Louis Public Library, then returned to the Decatur Public Library from 1909 to 1910. During 1910 to 1913, she was librarian of Milliken. From 1913 to 1917, she served as librarian of Wisconsin State Normal School. In 1918, she earned a B.L.S. degree from the University of Illinois and spent the remainder of her career on the Illinois Library School faculty.

Miss Boyd's keenest interest was in government publications. In 1931, she published a standard work, *United States Government Publications as Sources of Information for Libraries*. A revised edition appeared in 1949. Her book selection course at Illinois was regarded by students as a stimulating introduction to the world of books. She was widely esteemed as an inspiring teacher.

Miss Boyd was president of the Association of American Library Schools (1945) and vice-president of the Illinois Library Association (1928-1930). She retired in 1952 after thirty-two years on the Illinois faculty and died at age ninety.

BOYD, JULIAN PARKS (1903-1980) was born in Converse, South Carolina. He graduated *summa cum laude* from Duke University in 1925 and won a master's degree in political science from Duke the following year. He spent a year at the University of Pennsylvania in graduate work and as an assistant instructor. From 1932 to 1934, Boyd was director of the New York State Historical Association, followed by five years as librarian of the Historical Society of Pennsylvania. In 1940, he was appointed librarian of Princeton University and remained in that position until 1952. As librarian, he helped to plan the Firestone Memorial Library at Princeton, promoted a cooperative committee on library building plans, acted as a consultant to the Library of Congress, and was one of the originators of the Farmington Plan for the cooperative acquisition of foreign publications.

Boyd resigned his Princeton Library position in 1952 to concentrate full time on editing the Thomas Jefferson papers, a project that resulted in a multivolume edition. He served as professor of history at Princeton from 1952 to 1972, as president of the American Historical Association in 1964, and as president of the American Philosophical Society from 1973 to 1976.

BRADSHAW, LILLIAN MOORE (1915-   ) was born in Hagerstown, Maryland. She graduated from Western Maryland College in 1937 and earned a B.S. degree in library science from Drexel Institute in Philadelphia in 1938. The principal steps in her library career included assistant head of the Utica (New York) Public Library, 1941-1943; adult librarian at Baltimore's Enoch Pratt Library, 1943-1944; assistant coordinator of work with young adults, 1944-1946, at the same library; branch head at the Dallas Public Library, 1946; director of the Dallas Library readers' advisory service, 1947-1952; head of the Dallas Library circulation department, 1952-1955; coordinator of the Dallas Library adult service, 1955-1958; assistant director of the Dallas Library, 1958-1961; and director since 1961. In 1961-1962, she organized two bond issue campaigns that resulted in seven new branches of the Dallas Library.

In her library association activities, Mrs. Bradshaw was president of the Texas Library Association from 1964 to 1965 and president of the American Library Association from 1970 to 1971. According to one informed opinion, the Dallas Public Library developed under Mrs. Bradshaw from being called "the worst public library in the United States" into one of the best.

BRANSCOMB, LEWIS CAPERS, JR. (1911-   ) was born in Birmingham, Alabama. He graduated from Duke University in 1933 and from the University of Michigan Library School in 1941. He received a Ph.D. degree from the University of Chicago Graduate Library School in 1954. He was order librarian of the University of Georgia from 1939 to 1941, librarian of Mercer University from 1941 to 1942, librarian at the University of South Carolina from 1942 to 1944, and assistant director of the public service department at the University of Illinois from 1948 to 1952. From 1952 to 1971, he was director of libraries at Ohio State University in Columbus, and from 1971 to 1981, Branscomb was professor of Thurber Studies at Ohio State. He is a brother of Harvie Branscomb, once director of the Duke University Library and later president of Vanderbilt University.

BRAY, THOMAS (1656-1730) was born in Marton, Shropshire, England, and was educated at Oxford. In the seventeenth century, he began a movement to build large book collections, mainly theological in character, in the newly chartered colleges in colonial New England. Eventually, Bray was able to establish about fifty libraries in Maryland, New York, Pennsylvania, New Jersey, Boston, and the South. Some of the libraries continued until near the end of the eighteenth century. The Bray plan was also applied to England and Wales, where seventy-three libraries were founded.

BRETT, WILLIAM HOWARD (1846-1918) was born in Braceville, Ohio. His early interest in books was demonstrated by his becoming librarian of the Warren (Ohio) High School Library at age fourteen and clerking in a local bookstore. During the Civil War, he enrolled as a musician in the 196th Ohio Volunteer Infantry. Following the war, he was a student at the University of Michigan and at Western Reserve. For ten years, he was a clerk in a Cleveland bookstore. In 1884, he was chosen by the trustees of the Cleveland Public Library as librarian, a position that he held for thirty-four years.

Under Brett, the Cleveland Public Library developed into a great citywide system noted for its exceptional service, with a network of branches, stations, and school libraries. Brett also organized the Western Reserve University Library School and was its dean until his death. In 1895-1896, Brett organized and was the first president of the Ohio Library Association; he was president of the American Library Association in 1896-1897. Another contribution of Brett to librarianship was publication of the *Cumulative Index*, which later merged with the *Reader's Guide to Periodical Literature*.

A biography of Brett, *Portrait of a Librarian* (ALA, 1940), was published by another noted Cleveland librarian, Linda Eastman, in the American Library Pioneers series.

BRIGHAM, CLARENCE SAUNDERS (1877-1963) was born in Providence, Rhode Island, and graduated from Brown University in 1899. He began his library career immediately thereafter as an assistant on the Brown University Library staff. Beginning in 1900, he was for eight years librarian of the Rhode Island Historical Society. From 1908 to 1959, he was librarian of the American Antiquarian Society. Under Brigham's direction, the society developed major collections of manuscripts, maps, newspapers, prints, and other materials.

In 1913, Brigham undertook the tremendous task of compiling a bibliography and union list of early American newspapers. This project required thirty-two years to complete. The work first appeared serially in the *Proceedings of the American Antiquarian Society*, 1923-1927, and eventually was published in two volumes in 1947 under the title *History and Bibliography of American Newspapers, 1690-1820*. The compiler notes that the project "required travel of nearly 10,000 miles and examination of files in nearly four hundred towns and cities in thirty different states."

BRODERICK, DOROTHY M. (1929-   ) was born in Bridgeport, Connecticut. She graduated from New Haven State Teachers College in 1953 and from the Columbia Library School in 1956. She was a consultant for children's work in the New York State Library from 1960 to 1962 and joined the faculty of the Western Reserve Library School in 1963. In 1963 and 1964, she was editor of *Top of the News*. She also is the author of several books for children and of works relating to children's services in public libraries. She has assisted in the publication of several anthologies that have gained national attention and use. Broderick is a popular speaker in all areas of service to children and youth in the fields of books and their presentation.

BROWN, CHARLES HARVEY (1875-1960) was born in Albany, New York, and graduated from Wesleyan University. He also held a certificate from the New York State Library School. Beginning in 1901, he served for eighteen months as an assistant in the cataloging division of the Library of Congress. In 1903, he became a reference librarian on the John Crerar Library staff in Chicago, which gave him an opportunity to develop his lifelong interest in science and technology. His next move was to the Brooklyn Public Library as an assistant librarian in 1909. He remained there until 1919. For three years, beginning in 1919, he became a library specialist for the U.S. Navy and organized libraries on navy ships.

A major opportunity came for Brown in 1922, when he was appointed library director at Iowa State College, where over the next quarter century he developed one of the country's leading technological libraries. He built a strong staff and made frequent contributions to scientific and professional literature. Of first importance were Brown's *Land-Grant Survey* (1930) and *Circulation Work in College and University Libraries* (1933), with H. G. Bousfield. Some years later, in 1956, he published his highly influential work entitled *Scientific Serials*, a landmark in academic literature. In the field of professional librarianship, he organized the Association of Research Libraries in 1932 in cooperation with Windsor of Illinois, Leupp of California, Manchester of Ohio State, and Gerould of Princeton. In 1938, he helped to establish the Association of College and Reference Libraries as a division of the American Library Association, and he served as president of the ALA from 1941 to 1942. In 1947, Brown and Verner Clapp travelled to Japan to advise on the establishment of the National Diet Library.

A full-scale biography of Charles Harvey Brown by Edward G. Holley is nearing completion.

BROWN, WALTER LEWIS (1861-1931) was born in Buffalo, New York, and attended the Albany Academy. His library career began at the Young Men's Association Library in Buffalo, which was later called the Buffalo Library of Men, and then, in 1897, the Buffalo Public Library. In 1906, Brown was appointed librarian.

Brown was active in library associations. In 1906, he became president of the New York Library Association, and from 1916 to 1917, he served as president of the American Library Association. He died in 1931 in office.

BRYAN, HARRISON (1923-   ) was educated at the University of Queensland. He has become Australia's leading librarian, progressing from assistant librarian at the University of Queensland (1949-1950) to librarian of the University of Queensland (1950-1963). From 1963 to 1980, Bryan served as librarian of the University of Sydney, and in 1980, he became director of the National Library at Canberra. This appointment lasted until 1985. Bryan was a lieutenant in the Australian armed forces from 1942 to 1945. His writings include *Australian University Libraries Today and Tomorrow* (1965), *A Critical Survey of British University Libraries and Librarianship* (1966), and *University Libraries in Britain* (1976).

BRYAN, JAMES EDMUND (1909-   ) is a native of Easton, Pennsylvania. He graduated from Lafayette College at Easton in 1931, and the following year he received a degree in library science from Drexel Institute of Technology in Philadelphia. His first library job was as an assistant in the Washington (D.C.) Public Library in 1932, where he remained for four years working in the circulation, branch, science and technology, and acquisition departments. He earned a master's degree in political science at American University in 1937. His next position was librarian of the Easton Public Library from 1936 to 1938, after which he was appointed head of the adult lending department at the Carnegie Library of Pittsburgh for five years. In 1943, Bryan went to the Newark (New Jersey) Public Library as assistant director and succeeded John B. Kaiser as director in 1958.

As an expert on library sites and buildings, Bryan frequently has been called in as a consultant. He was president of the New

Jersey Library Association from 1952 to 1954 and president of the American Library Association from 1962 to 1963. He was presented with the Drexel Graduate School of Library Science Distinguished Achievement Award in 1963.

BRYANT, DOUGLAS WALLACE (1913-) was born in Visalia, California, and spent a year (1932-1933) at the University of Munich. He graduated from Stanford University in 1935 and from the Michigan Library School in 1938. He was an assistant in the Hoover Library at Stanford, 1934-1935; assistant curator of printed books at the Clements Library, University of Michigan, 1936-1938; senior reference assistant at the Detroit Public Library's Technical Department, 1938-1941; assistant chief of the Burton Historical Collection, 1941-1942; in the U.S. Navy, 1942-1946; assistant librarian at the University of California at Berkeley, 1946-1949; in the U.S. Information Service at the U.S. embassy in London, 1949-1952; assistant librarian at Harvard College, 1952-1956; associate director of the Harvard University Library and associate librarian of Harvard College, 1956-1964; university librarian at Harvard, 1964-1972; director of the university library and professor of bibliography at Harvard, 1972-1979; and librarian emeritus since in 1979. Bryant has had foreign assignments in London; Ankara, Turkey; Brussels; Berlin; and Tokyo.

BUCK, PAUL HERMAN (1899-1978) was born in Columbus, Ohio. He graduated from Ohio State University and held master's and doctoral degrees from Harvard. As a member of the history faculty at Harvard, he was an instructor from 1926 to 1936, an assistant professor from 1936 to 1939, and an associate professor from 1939 to 1942. In 1942, he became a professor and served in that capacity until 1969. He was dean of the faculty from 1942 to 1953 and provost from 1945 to 1953. From 1955 to 1964, Buck was director of university libraries at Harvard. He received many honors, including a Pulitzer Prize in history in 1938, and was decorated Chevalier of the French Legion of Honor.

BUTLER, PIERCE (1886-1953) was born in Clarendon Hills, Illinois. He held two degrees (in 1906 and 1910) from Dickinson College and a B.D. (1910) and Ph.D. (1912) from Hartford Theological Seminary. He became a reference assistant at the Newberry Library in Chicago in 1916 and was promoted to head the order department the following year. He began lecturing part-time on the history of printing at the University of Chicago in 1928 and joined the faculty of the Graduate Library School in 1931. He remained in that position until his retirement in 1952.

Butler's best-known work was *An Introduction to Library Science*, a work frequently cited in library schools. To his writing and teaching he brought a wide range of social, historical, and bibliographical knowledge. His death in 1953 resulted from an automobile accident that occurred while he was visiting lecturer at the University of North Carolina School of Library Science at Chapel Hill.

CAEN, JULIEN (1887-1974) was general administrator of the Bibliothèque Nationale, the French National Library, from 1930 to 1964. The printing of the library's alphabetical catalog, begun in 1896, continued under Caen. After World War II, Caen was appointed director of all French libraries.

CARNOVSKY, LEON (1903-1975) was born in St. Louis, Missouri. He graduated from the University of Missouri in 1927 and received a Ph.D. from the University of Chicago in 1932. His first job, in 1927-1928, was in the St. Louis Public Library, where he was a general assistant. From 1928 to 1929, he was assistant to the librarian at Washington University in St. Louis. His long-time association with the University of Chicago Graduate Library School began in 1932, when he was appointed an instructor. He rose successively through the various academic ranks until his retirement as professor emeritus in 1971. In addition, he served as assistant dean of the school from 1942 to 1945 and as associate dean and dean of students from 1945 to 1947. Carnovsky was a pioneer in library surveys and was responsible for many distinguished surveys, such as those of Westchester County (New York), Michigan State Library, Chicago Public Library, Cleveland Public Library, and Los Angeles Public Library.

Carnovsky's foreign assignments included serving as a member of the U.S. educational mission to Japan in 1946 and as UNESCO consultant to Israel in 1956 and to Greece in 1960. He also served as advisor to Japan, England, and the Soviet Union. Carnovsky was president of the Association of American Library Schools in 1942-1943. He was awarded the Melvil Dewey Medal in 1962, the Lippincott Award in 1975, and the Beta Phi Mu Award in 1971.

CARR, HENRY JAMES (1849-1929) was born in Pembroke, New Hampshire, and graduated from the University of Michigan Law School. He never practiced law, however, and instead became one of the early members of the American Library Association. In 1886, he was appointed librarian of the Grand Rapids (Michigan) Public Library. In the same year, he married Edith Wallbridge, Illinois state librarian. By 1890, he had converted the Grand Rapids Library into a modern, efficient institution. Carr then moved on to become chief librarian of the St. Joseph (Missouri) Public Library from 1890 to 1891. In 1891, he moved to Scranton, Pennsylvania, where he remained as public librarian until his death thirty-eight years later.

Carr was actively involved with the American Library Association, holding various offices until he became president in 1900-1901. Later, from 1907 to 1908, he was president of the Keystone Library Association.

CASTAGNA, EDWIN (1909-1983) was born in Petaluma, California, and worked at a variety of jobs before settling down.

He was a merchant seaman, a lumberjack, a ranch hand, a lumber camp worker, and a construction hand on the Coolidge Dam. He entered the University of California at Berkeley. Upon graduation, he enrolled in the School of Librarianship, and in 1936, he earned a certificate in librarianship. Further study took him to the University of Nevada at Reno, to Glendale College, and to Long Beach City College. In 1946-1947, he was president of the Nevada Library Association. His first important library post was as city librarian of the Long Beach (California) Public Library, where he remained for ten years. In September 1960, Castagna was appointed director of the Enoch Pratt Free Library in Baltimore, from which he retired in 1977. From 1964 to 1965, he was president of the American Library Association. The favorite occupation for Castagna and his wife was travel. They visited all parts of the continental United States, Hawaii, the South Pacific, Australia, Europe, Canada, North Africa, Cuba, Mexico, Guatemala, Peru, Ecuador, and Bolivia.

Castagna contracted an apparently incurable case of encephalitis. He and his wife Rachel were found dead from suicide in their Baltimore apartment.

CHAPIN, RICHARD E. (1925-   ) was born in Danville, Illinois. He graduated from Wabash College in 1948, holds two degrees from the University of Illinois Library School (1949 and 1955), and received a Ph.D. in communications from the University of Illinois in 1957. He served in the U.S. Navy from 1943 to 1946, during World War II. His library positions have included reference assistant at Florida State University, 1949-1950; circulation assistant at the University of Illinois Library, 1950-1953; assistant director of the University of Oklahoma School of Library Science, 1953-1955; and associate librarian of Michigan State University, 1955-1959. In 1959, he was appointed director of libraries at Michigan State University. He retired in 1989, after thirty years.

Chapin was president of the Michigan Library Association in 1966-1967 and chairman of the university libraries section of the

Association of College and Research Libraries in 1960. He has had foreign assignments in Brazil and Vietnam.

CHENEY, FRANCES NEEL (1906-) is recognized as one of the outstanding teachers of reference services. She was born in Washington, D.C. and graduated from Vanderbilt University. She holds library science degrees from Peabody and Columbia University. She was librarian of the chemistry department at Vanderbilt from 1928 to 1929, circulation librarian from 1929 to 1930, and reference librarian of the Joint University Libraries in Nashville, Tennessee, from 1930 to 1943. After a year at the Library of Congress, she returned to the Joint University Libraries as bibliographer in the general reference and bibliography division from 1944 to 1945 and as head of the department from 1945 to 1946. In 1946, she was appointed to the faculty of the Peabody Library School and served as associate director after 1960. In 1951-1952, she was a visiting professor in the Japan Library School at Keio University, Tokyo. She has been president of three divisions of the American Library Association: library education, reference services, and the American Association of School Librarians. She has also been president of the Southeastern Library Association and the Tennessee Library Association. In 1962, she received the Mudge Award, and in 1959, the Beta Phi Mu Good Teaching Award.

CLAPP, VERNER WARREN (1901-1977) was born in Johannesburg, South Africa, the son of an American businessman. He graduated from Trinity College in Hartford, Connecticut, in 1922. As a student, he was captain of the track team.

Clapp's first exposure to libraries was a summer job at the Library of Congress, in 1922, cataloging manuscripts. He took time out to do graduate work in philosophy at Harvard. In 1923, he returned for a permanent job at the Library of Congress. For the next thirty-three years, he was employed in succession as a member of the reference staff in the main reading room and as head of the congressional unit rooms, 1931-1937; as special assistant to the superintendent of the reading rooms, 1931-1937; as assistant superintendent of that division, 1937-1940; as administrative assistant to the librarian of Congress and director of the administrative department, 1940-1943; and as director of the acquisitions department, 1943-1947. When the United Nations Conference on International Organization met in San Francisco in 1945, Clapp was asked to set up a library to serve the conference. The present United Nations Library in New York evolved from that undertaking.

In March 1947, Clapp was appointed chief assistant librarian of Congress. Later, in the same year, he was chairman of the U.S. library mission to Japan, a move that led to the establishment of the National Diet Library in Tokyo.

In 1956, the Ford Foundation made a grant to establish the Council on Library Resources. Clapp resigned his position at the Library of Congress to become the first president of the council. The council's announced aims, through grants, was to seek solutions to library problems "through basic research, the development of new techniques and equipment, and through coordination of effort."

Clapp's former colleagues at the Library of Congress noted "his insatiable curiosity and his inexhaustible energies, his skill as a diplomat, his inventiveness, his instinct for leadership, and his undaunted spirit."

CLEMONS, HENRY (1879-1968) was born in Corry, Pennsylvania. He graduated from Wesleyan University in 1902 and earned a master's degree from Princeton in 1905. He was a student at Oxford University from 1906 to 1907 and at the Columbia School of Library Service in 1937. His library career began as an assistant at Wesleyan in 1902-1903. From 1908 to 1913, he was a reference librarian at Princeton, and from 1927 to 1950, he was librarian of the University of Virginia. In 1913-1920, he was professor of English at the University of Nanking (China), and he served there as librarian from 1914 to 1927. Another of Clemons's foreign assignments was to represent the ALA in charge of library war service, American Expeditionary Force, Siberia, 1918-1919. In 1922, he served as special cataloger in the Chinese section of the Library of Congress. Clemons was president of the Virginia Library Association in 1931-1932 and received the University of Virginia's Thomas Jefferson Award in 1956.

CLIFT, DAVID HORACE (1907-1973) was born in Washington, Kentucky. He graduated from the University of Kentucky in 1930 and from the School of Library Service at Columbia University in 1931. In his junior year in college, he was employed as a student assistant at the university library and for summer work at the Lexington Public Library. While at Columbia, he was also a student worker in the library. His first professional job was as a reference assistant at the New York Public Library from 1931 to 1937. He then became assistant to the director of the Columbia University libraries, 1937-1942. Three years of military service during World War II, from 1942 to 1945, were spent in the U.S. Army's Office of Strategic Servics.

From 1945 to 1951, Clift was associate librarian of Yale University. In 1951, he succeeded John Mackenzie Cory as executive secretary (and after 1958, he became executive director) of the American Library Association until his sudden death in 1973. Among the highlights of his career were serving as president of the New York Library Club from 1941 to 1942, as president of the Connecticut Library Association from 1950 to 1951, as chief of the Library of Congress mission to Germany from 1945 to 1946, as head of a delegation of U.S. librarians on a study tour of the Soviet Union in 1961, as a delegate to the International Federation of Library Associations from 1964 to 1972, and as a contributor to the Japan–U.S. Conference on Libraries and Information Science in Higher Education in Tokyo in 1969.

Clift was an active leader in the ALA fight for intellectual freedom. During his administration, the association created the Office for Intellectual Freedom, with Judith F. Krug as director.

Among the many honors received by Clift were the Lippincott Award for distinguished library service (1962) and election to honorary life membership in the ALA (1972).

COLE, GEORGE WATSON (1850-1939), the first librarian of the Huntington Library, was born in Warren, Connecticut. In 1888, he graduated from Melvil Dewey's School of Library Economy at Columbia University. A series of jobs followed: he worked at libraries in Fitchburg, Massachusetts, from 1885 to 1886, and in Brooklyn, New York, from 1886 to 1887. From 1888 to 1890, he was an assistant to William Poole at the Newberry Library in Chicago, and from 1891 to 1895, he was librarian of the Jersey City Public Library. He also was a bibliographer in the Lenox Library (New York) under Wilberforce Eames. Cole's most important assignment came in 1915, when he was appointed librarian of the Henry E. Huntington Library in San Marino, California. He remained in that position until 1924 and was placed in charge of the most comprehensive private library ever assembled on American and British history and literature, acquired by Huntington through a number of great private collections. Cole's expert knowledge and experience were major assets in the development of a notable research library.

Cole was president of the Bibliographical Society of America from 1916 to 1921.

COMPTON, CHARLES HERRICK (1880-1966) was born in Palmyra, Nebraska, and graduated from the University of Nebraska in 1901. After several miscellaneous jobs, he enrolled under Melvil Dewey at the New York State Library School in 1905 and received a B.L.S. degree in 1908. He started his career as librarian of the University of North Dakota. He spent the next ten years, starting in 1910, as reference librarian of the Seattle Public Library, under Judson T. Jennings. He spent the World War I years in Washington assisting the ALA's Library War Service, under Herbert Putnam.

He returned to Seattle for a short time but in 1921 accepted an appointment, under Arthur Bostwick, as assistant librarian of the St. Louis Public Library. In 1938, he succeeded Bostwick as librarian.

Compton followed Gratia A. Countryman as president of the American Library Association for 1934-1935. He had served previously as president of the Missouri Library Association. He was the ALA's representative at the 1935 International Library Congress in Spain.

CONEY, DONALD (1901-1973) was born in Jackson, Michigan, and held degrees, including an A.M. in library science, from the University of Michigan. His professional experience began with various positions on the University of Michigan staff from 1920 to 1927. In 1927-1928, he was librarian of the University of Delaware; from 1928 to 1931, he served as assistant librarian of the University of North Carolina. In 1931-1932, Coney was professor of library science and assistant director of the University of North Carolina Library School, and from 1932 to 1934, he was in charge of technical processes for the Newberry Library in Chicago. He was a librarian for the University of Texas from 1934 to 1945 and librarian and professor of librarianship at the University of California at Berkeley from 1945 until his death in 1973. He also taught at the University of Chicago Graduate Library School and at the University of Illinois Library School. In 1941-1942, Coney was the fourth president of the Association of College and Research Libraries.

COTTON DES HOUSSAYES, JEAN-BAPTISTE (1727-1783) was born in Normandy near Rouen. In 1776, he went to Paris, where he became librarian of the Sorbonne for seven years until his death. He wrote a long discourse, published in Latin, French, and English, on the duties and qualifications of a librarian, and he explored the history of librarianship since the Renaissance. He particularly admired two cardinals, Quirini (1680-1759) and Passionei (1682-1761); and former librarians of the Vatican, Gabriel Naudé, creator of the Mazarine Library, and Ludovico Antonio Muratori (1672-1750), librarian of the ducal court of Modena. In his writings, Cotton insisted that a librarian should possess vast knowledge, be expert in bibliography and book selection, and be prepared to welcome all scholars.

COULTER, EDITH MARGARET (1880-1963) was born in Salinas, California. She graduated from Stanford in 1905 and enrolled in the New York State Library School course at Albany for two years. Returning to California, she was on the staff of the Berkeley Public Library, of Stanford University, and of the University of California at Berkeley. After the establishment of the Graduate School of Librarianship at Berkeley, she joined Sidney Mitchell on the faculty. She served as president of the ALA College and Reference Section from 1924 to 1925 and was president of the American Association of Library Schools from 1942 to 1943. Coulter received the ALA's Isadore Gilbert Award for distinguished work in reference librarianship in 1961 and won an honorary doctorate from Mills College in 1960.

COUNTRYMAN, GRATIA ALTA (1866-1953) was born in Hastings, Minnesota, and graduated from the University of Minnesota in 1889. She began in 1889 as an assistant in the newly established Minneapolis Public Library, then under Herbert Putnam's direction. She was soon promoted to head of the catalog department and two years later was appointed assistant librarian. In 1904, she succeeded James K. Hosmer as chief librarian, a position that she held until 1936. Under her energetic direction, library service expanded into all areas of the city and into Hennepin County. The Hennepin County Library was established in 1922, with Gratia Countryman as county librarian.

Miss Countryman was active in professional organizations. She was elected to the American Library Institute in 1906 and became president of the American Library Association for 1933-1934. In

1935, she was an ALA delegate to the Second International Library and Bibliographic Congress in Madrid.

CRANE, EVAN JAY (1889-1966) was born in Columbus, Ohio, and graduated from Ohio State University in 1914. His career focused on chemical literature. He served for forty-four years, from 1914 to 1958, as editor of *Chemical Abstracts*, establishing it as the standard work in its field. Crane was an active author and contributed numerous articles to chemical periodicals. He was recognized by chemical societies for his achievements and received an honorary doctor of science degree from Ohio State University.

CRAVER, HARRISON WARWICK (1875-1951) was born in Owaneco, Illinois, and graduated from Rose Polytechnic Institute at Terre Haute, Indiana, in 1895. He was employed in industry until 1902, when he became technology librarian of the Carnegie Library of Pittsburgh. In 1908, he was appointed librarian. His next move, the final one, was to the position of director of the Engineering Societies Library in New York City, where Craver remained until his retirement in 1945. The Engineering Societies Library was sponsored and maintained by four major engineering organizations. Under Craver's direction, it became the premier library in the country in engineering and technology. The entire collection was cataloged and classified by Margaret Mann, as head of the library's catalog department.

Craver was active in the affairs of professional library associations. He served as president of the Keystone Library Association from 1908 to 1909, of the New York Library Club from 1921 to 1922, and of the American Library Association from 1937 to 1938.

CRISMOND, LINDA (1943-   ) was born in Burbank, California. On September 1, 1989, she became the nineteenth executive director of the American Library Association, the first woman to become executive director since the ALA was established in 1876.

For nine years, she was director of the Los Angeles County Library. Previously, from 1973 to 1980, she was assistant librarian of the University of Southern California, and from 1965 to 1973, she held various positions with the San Francisco Public Library.

CROSLAND, DOROTHY MURRAY (1903-1983) was born in Stone Mountain, Georgia, and received a certificate in library science from Atlanta University in 1923. Her first library experience was in the Atlanta Public Library as a catalog assistant from 1922 to 1925 and as a branch librarian in 1925. Her long and distinguished career with the Georgia Institute of Technology began as assistant librarian, 1925-1926, and continued from 1927 until her retirement as director. She was president of the Georgia Library Association from 1949 to 1951 and of the Southeastern Library Association from 1952 to 1954. As head of the Georgia Tech Library, Mrs. Crosland supervised the construction of a central library building and developed outstanding collections in science and engineering. She was named Atlanta Woman of the Year in Education in 1945.

CRUNDEN, FREDERICK MORGAN (1847-1911) was born in Gravesend, England. In his early childhood, his parents moved to St. Louis, Missouri, where he earned two degrees at Washington University between 1868 and 1872. In 1877, he was appointed librarian of the Public School Library. In that position, he actively promoted the idea of a free public library tax supported by and separate from the school board. Before he died, St. Louis had a great public library with six branches. Crunden was vice-president in 1887 and president from 1889 to 1890, of the American Library Association; the first president of the Missouri Library Association; vice-president of the International Library Conference; and chairman of the library section of the Louisiana Purchase Exposition.

CULVER, ESSAE MARTHA (1881-1973) was born in Emporia, Kansas. She graduated from Pomona College in Claremont,

California, in 1904, and attended the New York State Library School in 1908. From 1909 to 1912, she was librarian of the Salem (Oregon) Public Library. From 1912 to 1925, she was successively librarian of the Glenn, Butte, and Merced county libraries and library visitor for the California State Library.

On the recommendation of Milton J. Ferguson, California state librarian, Miss Culver was appointed executive secretary of the Louisiana Library Commission in 1925. It was a strategic moment. With support from a Carnegie Corporation grant, Louisiana was on the verge of a major expansion in statewide library development. Miss Culver's efforts were directed first at the creation of a strong central reference library to serve the state government and libraries around the state, and second, at the establishment of public libraries to reach all state citizens. She also encouraged the development of a strong school library program in the State Department of Education. When Miss Culver retired in 1962, after thirty-seven years of service, all of these goals had been achieved substantially.

Essae Martha Culver was active in library organizations. She was president of the Louisiana Library Association, 1928-1929; of the Southwestern Library Association, 1936-1938; of the League of Library Commissions, 1931-1933; and of the American Library Association, 1940-1941. The ALA presented her with the Lippincott Award in 1959, and in 1962, the Louisiana Library Association established the Essae M. Culver Award for distinguished service to librarianship.

CUNNINGHAM, EILEEN RETCH (1894-1965) was born in Baltimore and married a physician from the Vanderbilt University Medical School at Nashville. She became librarian of the Vanderbilt Medical Library in 1929, a position that she held for twenty-seven years. She was an active member of the Medical Library Association, attended an International Congress on Libraries and Bibliography in Madrid, surveyed medical libraries in Colombia and Mexico for the Rockefeller Corporation, reorganized the medical library in Lima, Peru, was elected president of the Medical Library Association in 1947, and developed a widely used classification for medical literature. By 1949, she had become "perhaps the best known medical librarian in the world." She retired in 1956 but remained active in various undertakings until her death in 1965.

CUTTER, CHARLES AMMI (1837-1903) entered Harvard College at age fourteen and graduated third among eighty-two members of the class of 1855. He was a student and librarian at Harvard Divinity School and then went on to the Harvard Library, where he served as assistant librarian from 1860 to 1868. In 1868, Cutter was elected librarian of the Boston Athenaeum, where he worked with several noted directors and provided library service for leading New England authors. Over a period of twelve years, he produced the monumental *Catalogue of the Library of the Boston Athenaeum* (five volumes, 1874-1882). Also, in 1875, he published his *Rules for a Printed Dictionary Catalogue*, which became a leading textbook in systematic dictionary cataloging. Cutter was president of the American Library Association from 1887 to 1889, helped to establish the *Library Journal* in 1876, and was its editor from 1881 to 1893. One of his well-known works is *Expansive Classification* (1891-1894). Most widely used are his *Rules* and alphabetic-order tables for the names of authors, still in general use in American libraries.

DALTON, JACK (1908-) was born in Holland, Virginia, and was a student at Virginia Polytechnic Institute from 1924 to 1927, majoring in chemical engineering. From 1927 to 1930, he attended the University of Virginia and received a B.S. degree in English literature. He earned an M.S. degree in library science at the University of Michigan in 1936. From 1934 to 1942, he was reference librarian, and from 1942 to 1956 associate librarian, at the University of Virginia. He served as librarian from 1950 to 1956. He became director of the ALA International Relations Office in Chicago from 1956 to 1959, during which he engaged in worldwide travel. In 1959, Dalton was appointed dean of Columbia University's School of Library Service and served in that position until 1970. From 1970 to 1979, Dalton was director of the Library Development Center. He has been a consultant and advisor to various institutions and foundations.

DANA, JOHN COTTON (1856-1929) was a dynamic personality who won fame as a public librarian, museum director, author, printer, and president of the American Library Association (1895-1896). He was a graduate of Dartmouth College, was admitted to the New York bar in 1883, and early in his career worked as a civil engineer and newspaper man. In 1889, Dana was appointed librarian of the Denver Public Library and over a period of eight years transformed that institution, including establishment of a children's department. In 1898, he went on to become librarian of the Springfield (Massachusetts) Public Library, with similar dramatic results. His greatest impact was on the Newark (New Jersey) Public Library, of which he was appointed librarian in 1902. Under his administration, there were large increases in the book collection and in home circulation, and branch libraries were opened throughout the city, including the famous Business Branch located in the financial and commercial district. As founder and director of the Newark Museum, he achieved similar success. He and his brother established the Elm Tree Press at Woodstock. One commentator noted, "On everything he touched he left the stamp of a unique personality."

DANTON, J. PERIAM (1908-   ) was born in Palo Alto, California, and graduated from Oberlin College in 1925. He was a student at the University of Leipzig from 1925 to 1926 and received a B.L.S. degree from Columbia in 1929. In 1930, he earned an

M.A. in German from Williams College, followed by a Ph.D. from Chicago's Graduate Library School in 1935. He was a reference assistant at Williams, 1929-1930; ALA assistant, 1930-1933; librarian of Colby College, 1935-1936; and librarian of Temple University, 1936-1942. During World War II, he served with the U.S. Naval Reserves in the Pacific area from 1942 to 1945. Danton was dean of the School of Librarianship at the University of California at Berkeley from 1946 to 1961 and thereafter was a member of the faculty. He has held a variety of assignments abroad for UNESCO and the U.S. State Department in Germany, Austria, Norway, and Jamaica and has written extensively on library education and international librarianship.

DAVID, CHARLES WENDELL (1890-1989) was born in Onarga, Illinois. He graduated from Oxford University as a Rhodes scholar in 1911 and received a doctorate from Harvard in 1918. After periods of teaching history at the University of Washington and Bryn Mawr College, he became professor of history and the first full-time director of libraries at the University of Pennsylvania, from 1940 to 1955. For the next fifteen years, he achieved a remarkable transformation of the libraries, revitalizing and expanding them. He played a key role in the development of the Union Library Catalog of the Philadelphia Metropolitan Area. He also served a five-year term as executive secretary of the Association of Research Libraries.

After his retirement from the University of Pennsylvania in 1955, David planned and established the Eleutherian Mills Historical Library at Longwood, Delaware, 1955-1961, and the Mystic Seaport Museum in Connecticut, 1962. He died at age ninety-nine.

DAVIS, RAYMOND CAZALLIS (1836-1919), born in Cushing, Maine, is viewed as one of the pioneers of the library movement in America. He entered the University of Michigan as a student in 1855 after a round-the-world voyage with his father. In 1868, he was appointed assistant librarian at the University of Michigan, a position that he held for four years. In 1877, he became librarian at the university, starting a remarkably successful stay of twenty-eight years, from 1887 to 1905. The library's book collection grew rapidly under his direction, making it one of the country's most important libraries. Davis also gave lectures on bibliography in 1887 at the newly established School of Library Economy at Columbia University, the first such school in the United States, started by Melvil Dewey.

DE GENNARO, RICHARD (1926-   ) was born in New Haven, Connecticut. He holds degrees from Wesleyan University and Columbia (in library science) and did graduate study (1951-1955) in Paris, Madrid, and Perugia. He was also enrolled in the advanced management program at Harvard in 1971. He was appointed reference librarian of the New York Public Library from 1956 to 1958, and from 1987 to 1990 was director of that institution. In June 1990, De Gennaro returned to Harvard University as the Roy E. Larsen Librarian of Harvard College. Previously, from 1958 to 1970, he was on the Harvard University Library staff, and from 1970 to 1986, he was director of libraries at the University of Pennsylvania. His professional activities have included the presidency of the Association of Research Libraries, 1975, and of the ALA Information Science and Automation Division. He was winner of the Melvil Dewey Medal in 1986.

DELISLE, LEOPOLD VICTOR (1824-1910) joined the Bibliothèque Nationale, the French national library in Paris, in 1852 and remained with it for fifty-two years. For thirty-one years, he was the library's general director. Through various measures, the library's collections grew enormously during that period. Delisle's chief work as a librarian was to develop a catalog of the Bibliothèque Nationale's manuscripts that was published in 1868-1881 in three volumes. He also edited and published many volumes of manuscripts, relating chiefly to the Middle Ages.

DEWEY, MELVIL (1851-1931) was the founder of library science and of education for librarianship in America. He was a truly dynamic, complex, and versatile character. His major achievements included the creation of the Dewey decimal classification, used in libraries around the world, the founding of the American Library Association, the establishment of the first school for the preparation of professional librarians, and inauguration of the *Library Journal*, the first periodical devoted to library affairs. Further, Dewey took the lead in advocating school library services and became the leading state librarian in America, one of the most prominent academic librarians of his time, and an active library entrepreneur.

If those achievements were not sufficient, Dewey was a central figure in a number of other social movements, such as the American Metric Bureau, the Spelling Reform Association, and the Lake Placid Club.

Dewey's interest in libraries began early. He entered Amherst College in 1870, graduating in 1874. During his junior year, he was employed in the college library and served as acting librarian for a short time after graduation. Thus was launched his notable career in librarianship. From the outset, Dewey was appalled by the lack of efficiency in library management. At the time, libraries normally arranged their collections by a fixed location scheme; a book's location was fixed on a specific shelf in a specific section or range of shelves. This meant that works on the same subject were not shelved together, and any building expansion required extensive shifting and numbering on books and in catalogs — an expensive process.

To clarify his own ideas about more efficient operation of libraries, Dewey planned visits to more than fifty libraries in New York and New England. On the basis of his observations, he conceived the idea of relative location and a system of classification, the principal features of which should be that it would be simple to use, would be universally applicable, and would not be changed constantly. The first fruit of his inspiration was publication in 1876 of Dewey's *A Classification and Subject Index for Cataloguing and Arranging the Books and Pamphlets of a Library*. He presented the scheme to the Amherst Library committee and received permission to use it in the Amherst Library.

Thus was born the Dewey decimal classification, one of Dewey's major contributions to library science. The system assigns an appropriate identifying number to every book, thereby making it easier to arrange and to find books on the library shelves. The system is devised to bring all books on the same subject together and related subjects nearby. It divides all books into ten main classes with an infinite number of subgroups. Since its original publication, the Dewey decimal classification has gone through numerous editions, has been expanded constantly to recognize new fields and changing subjects, and is used worldwide.

In 1876, Dewey went to Boston. There he took an active part in preparing for the conference of librarians to be held in Philadelphia in October. The meeting led to the founding of the American Library Association. Dewey served as secretary of the conference and remained as secretary until 1890. He was elected to two terms as ALA president, from 1890 to 1893, and served for three terms as treasurer. In effect, Dewey was the motivating force for beginning the American Library Association, and he dominated the organization for thirty years.

In the same year as the birth of the American Library Association, 1876, Dewey began editorship of the *Library Journal*, which he believed was a second essential step in establishing librarianship as a profession. The aim of the new periodical was to "cover the entire field of library and bibliographical interests." Later, in 1886, Dewey established another journal, *Library Notes*, designed to reach small libraries with information on recent developments of concern to them.

Moving next into a field that Dewey recognized was of great practical importance to libraries, for two years, 1877-1878, he used his office to test library supplies and equipment. In 1882,

Dewey set up the Library Bureau and remained as head of the firm for twenty-five years. He was always ready to try new materials and methods, as shown by his adoption of the typewriter, the telephone, and other mechanical improvements. One biographer, John P. Comaromi, noted that Dewey "would have equally easily adopted the computer if he were working now."

Dewey always preferred the company of women to men, and his working relationships with women generally ran far more smoothly than his relationships with men. In 1878, he married Annie Godfrey, then librarian of Wellesley College, who remained his companion and advisor for the next half century.

Columbia University (then Columbia College) gave Dewey the opportunity to test his library theories, show his administrative ability, and establish the first professional field for librarians. The Columbia trustees were looking for a library leader who would bring fresh ideas, provide central direction and control of the college's scattered collections, and improve the library's service functions. Prior to his appointment, Dewey appeared before a trustees' committee on the library to present his views on how the library should be organized and managed and to give his proposal for a library school. The trustees were impressed, and with strong backing from President Frederick Barnard, Dewey was appointed librarian-in-chief for three years at a salary of $3,500 a year. It was destined to be a stormy period in Dewey's career.

Dewey attacked Columbia's library problems with his usual inexhaustible energy and enthusiasm. Completion of a new building provided a chance for more efficient library administration. Collections from a number of separate libraries were brought together under central control; all were sorted, weeded, classified, and cataloged. Serious deficiencies in the library's holdings were corrected by new acquisitions, with the cooperation of the faculty. The Dewey decimal classification, of course, was used. A key element — one of Dewey's primary objectives — was to make the Columbia library of maximum usefulness to faculty, students, and the community. To that end, he publicized long hours of opening, including vacation periods, holidays, and evenings, and invited use by townspeople. The library became a center for meetings of groups such as the New York Library Club (formed by Dewey), the National Sunday School Library Union, and the Children's Library Association.

Dewey raised a storm at Columbia in 1887 when he started a School of Library Economy; seventeen of the first twenty students to matriculate in the first class were women, contrary to the university's regulations. The following year, 1888, the trustees voted to suspend Dewey from his duties in the library. The ostensible reason concerned a questionnaire in which applicants for admission to the library school were asked to state their height, weight, and color of hair and eyes, and to send a photograph — all of which the trustees thought objectionable. A few weeks later, Dewey resigned.

Almost immediately, he found a new field for his efforts. The regents of the University of the State of New York offered him the position of director of the state library. Dewey plunged into action at once and over the next several years brought the library to greatly increased usefulness. He developed the collections and demonstrated the possibilities of the home education department, the extension division, the traveling libraries, and the library school. The school that he had started at Columbia — the first in the United States — moved to Albany with Dewey and soon gained a reputation for being the leading institution in its field. The Association of State Librarians and the New York Library Association were organized, with Dewey playing a leading role. Throughout his approximately seventeen years in Albany, Dewey worked with incredible energy. Special collections and services were developed for medicine, for the blind, and for women and children, and the library's operations and services expanded in almost every conceivable direction. Dewey's primary objective was to extend the library's role in the schools, colleges, cities, and states.

Unfortunately, Dewey's somewhat abrasive personality created a number of powerful enemies. Although charges of financial irregularities were made against him, investigations cleared him of these charges. In 1904, however, Andrew S. Draper, former president of the University of Illinois, a man apparently as power-hungry as Dewey, and who probably was jealous of Dewey, was appointed to head the New York State Education Department. Draper did not admire Dewey, believed that Dewey had overestimated the importance of libraries, and wanted to strengthen the position of schools at the expense of libraries. Dewey's position under Draper gradually became untenable, and in 1906, Dewey resigned as New York state librarian. This was the effective end of his career as a librarian, at the age of fifty-four.

The remaining years of Dewey's life were spent in developing the Lake Placid Club in the Adirondacks, which had been incorporated in 1896 as a membership social club. The organization's rate of growth under the direction of Dewey and his wife was phenomenal. It became a multimillion-dollar enterprise, with thousands of members. An equally prosperous branch was the Lake Placid Club in Florida, where the Deweys spent their winters. Controversy followed Dewey in the Lake Placid Club, too. Anti-semitism was charged in the choice of guests invited to visit and use the club.

A distinguished public librarian, Frank P. Hill, a contemporary of Dewey, described Melvil Dewey as "the most influential and effective librarian who ever dwelt among us." The sum of Dewey's accomplishments would seem fully to justify such a superlative rating.

DICKINSON, ASA DON (1876-1960) was born in Detroit. His thirty-five years in the library profession were spent as assistant librarian of the Brooklyn Public Library, 1903-1906; as librarian of Union College in Schenectady, New York, 1907-1909; as librarian of the Leavenworth (Kansas) Public Library, 1907-1909; as librarian of Washington State College in Pullman, 1909-1912;

and as librarian at the University of the Punjab for the Indian government in Lahore, 1915-1916. He became librarian of the University of Pennsylvania from 1919 to 1931. His last appointment was as librarian of Brooklyn College from 1931 to 1944.

Dickinson is best known for authoring *The World's Best Books*, 1948 and 1953, a widely known and used compilation.

DIX, WILLIAM SHEPHERD (1910-1978) was born in Winchester, Virginia. He graduated from the University of Virginia and earned a doctorate from the University of Chicago. His early career involved positions teaching English at Western Reserve University, Williams College, Harvard, and Rice University, from 1940 to 1948. In 1948, he was appointed director of the Rice Library. There he soon achieved a leadership position among the nation's university and research libraries. He became librarian of Princeton University in 1953; president of the American Library Association in 1969-1970; executive secretary of the Association of College and Research Libraries; vice-chairman of the U.S. Commission to UNESCO, 1958-1960; chairman of the ALA International Relations Committee, 1955-1960; and chairman of the ALA Intellectual Freedom Committee, 1951-1953, from which vantage point he was principal author of ALA's celebrated "Freedom to Read" statement in 1953.

In naming Dix as Man of the Week in 1959, the *Princeton Town Topics* stated: "For understanding and stressing that books are among our greatest instruments for freedom; for seeing that the American library is an invaluable weapon in the arsenal of democracy . . . Dix has enabled others to see that the unregimented library is all important when it comes to promoting the free flow of ideas."

DOMS, KEITH (1920-) was born in Endeavor, Wisconsin. He graduated from the University of Wisconsin in 1942 and received a B.L.S. degree from the University of Wisconsin Library School in 1947. In between, he served in the U.S. Army and was a student for nine months at the school of Far Eastern Studies at Harvard.

At the beginning of his library career, Doms was city librarian in Concord, New Hampshire, 1947-1951; librarian of the Midland (Michigan) Public Library, 1951-1956; and assistant director and later associate director of the Carnegie Library of Pittsburgh, 1956-1964. He was elected president of the Pennsylvania Library Association in 1961. In 1964, he was appointed director of the Carnegie Library, and in that position he built three main branch buildings, established a program to provide technical and scientific literature to business and industry, set up a library program for juvenile delinquents, expanded services for the blind, and began a mobile library for disadvantaged neighborhoods. In 1964, Doms went to Karachi, Pakistan, at the request of the U.S. State Department to promote public library development.

In 1969, Doms succeeded Emerson Greenaway as director of the Free Library of Philadelphia. He has long been active in the American Library Association and served as ALA president in 1971-1972. He was awarded the Pennsylvania Library Association's Award of Merit and was president from 1963 to 1964 of Beta Phi Mu, the national honorary library fraternity.

He retired from the Philadelphia Free Library in 1987 and became executive director of the Urban Libraries Council in Philadelphia. He received the Lippincott Award in 1982.

DOUGHERTY, RICHARD MARTIN (1935-) was born in East Chicago, Indiana, graduated from Purdue University in 1959, and received M.L.S. and Ph.D. degrees in library science from Rutgers University between 1961 and 1963. From 1963 to 1966, he was chief of the acquisitions department at the University of North Carolina, and from 1966 to 1970, he was associate director at the University of Colorado libraries. He became a professor of library science at Syracuse University from 1970 to 1972 and served as university librarian at the University of California at Berkeley from 1972 to 1978. Since 1978, he has been director of libraries at the University of Michigan in Ann Arbor. Dougherty was editor of *College and Research Libraries* from 1969 to 1974 and is the author of *Scientific Management of Library Organizations* (1983). He was named Academic Librarian of the Year in 1983 by the Association of College and Research Libraries and was elected president of the American Library Association for the 1990-1991 term.

DOUGLAS, MARY TERESA PEACOCK (1903-1970) was born in Salisbury, North Carolina, and graduated from the University of North Carolina at Greensboro in 1923. She received a B.S. in library science from Columbia's School of Library Service in 1931. After a preliminary period of teaching and serving as a school librarian, she became the first state school library advisor in the North Carolina Department of Public Instruction, where she made notable contributions to school library development in the state, in the South, and in the nation. Several widely used handbooks were published under her direction, and she traveled extensively to promote school library standards and library education for school librarians.

In recognition of her professional leadership, Mrs. Douglas served as chairman of the school and children's section of the North Carolina Library Association and of the school libraries section of the Southeastern Library Association from 1937 to 1938. She was president of the North Carolina Library Association in 1939-1941, chairman of the American Library Association's school libraries section in 1943-1944, president of ALA's division of libraries for children and young people in 1944-1945, and chairman of the national organization of State School Library Supervisors in 1946-1947. Mrs. Douglas left state supervision in 1947 to become the first supervisor of libraries in the Raleigh (North Carolina) City Schools and continued in that position until her retirement in 1968. In cooperation with teachers, librarians, and administrators, she led the development of an outstanding program of library service. Her influence was exerted through her publications, such as the *Teacher-Librarian's Handbook* (ALA, 1941 and 1949), which sold more than 50,000 copies and was translated into a number of foreign languages; through her work with the Southern Association of Colleges and Schools in establishing school library standards; through her teaching in summer schools and workshops in various colleges and universities; and through her speaking to many education and library associations.

Mrs. Douglas received the Grolier Society Award in 1958 for her contributions; a new elementary school in Raleigh was named for her in 1968; and the Mary Peacock Douglas Award was established by the North Carolina Library Association, also in 1968, to honor her outstanding contributions to school libraries in the state. Until her death in 1970, she continued to read to groups of children and to encourage the practice of storytelling in schools and libraries.

Downs, Jane Bliss (1914-   ) is a graduate of Duke University (1934) and holds an M.A. in American literature from Duke (1944) and a B.A.L.S. from the University of North Carolina (1937). She was on the staff of the Detroit Public Library from 1937 to 1940, served as director of libraries for Durham (North Carolina) City Schools from 1942 to 1968, and was children's consultant for the North Carolina State Library from 1968 to 1974. She is the author of *The Story Experience* (1978) and *Children's Writings* (1982). She was given the Grolier Award in 1975 and served as president of the North Carolina Library Association from 1952 to 1954.

Downs, Robert Bingham (1903-   ), a native of North Carolina, is a graduate of the University of North Carolina and of the Columbia School of Library Service. He holds six honorary doctorates. After serving as a student assistant under Louis Round Wilson at Chapel Hill, he worked for two years as a reference librarian at the New York Public Library, 1927-1929; as librarian of Colby College, 1929-1931; as assistant librarian and then librarian of the University of North Carolina, 1931-1938; as director of libraries at New York University, 1938-1943; and as director, then dean, of the University of Illinois Library and Library School, 1943-1971. Foreign missions have taken him to Japan, Turkey, Afghanistan, Mexico, Australia, New Zealand, Tunisia, Canada, and Britain. He has served as president of the Association of College and Research Libraries (1940-1941), the Illinois Library Association (1955-1956), and the American Library Association (1952-1953). He is the author of more than 400 books, articles, and reviews. His autobiography, *Perspectives on the Past*, was published in 1984.

In 1929, Downs married Elizabeth Crooks, a 1927 graduate of the Columbia Library School and a member of the Columbia University departmental library staff. In 1983, he was married to Jane Bliss Wilson, whose career included a lengthy period as a school and children's librarian in Detroit and North Carolina, as a member of the North Carolina State Library staff, as president of the North Carolina Library Association, and as a winner of the Grolier Award in 1975.

DRURY, FRANCIS KEESE WYNKOOP (1878-1954) was born in Ghent, New York, and graduated from Rutgers University and the University of Illinois Library School. He held several positions at the University of Illinois from 1905 to 1919, was assistant librarian of Brown University from 1919 to 1929, and served as executive assistant for adult education with the American Library Association from 1929 to 1931. In 1931, Drury became librarian of the Nashville (Tennessee) Public Library and remained in that position until his retirement in 1946. At the same time, he was visiting lecturer at the Peabody Library School. At Nashville, he established a business branch, as well as special stations to serve minority groups, he expanded the library to encompass county-wide service, and he initiated a bookmobile service.

Drury wrote extensively on book selection, reading, drama, and order work in libraries.

DUDGEON, MATTHEW SIMPSON (1871-1949) was born in Madison, Wisconsin, and graduated from Baker University in 1892. He became secretary of the Wisconsin Free Library Commission, from which he directed the University of Wisconsin Library School, administered traveling libraries for more than 1,500 rural communities, and advised the state's public libraries. In 1919-1920, he served as director of domestic camp libraries for the ALA's Library War Service. In 1921, Dudgeon was appointed director of the Milwaukee Public Library, a post that he held for twenty-one years. Under his leadership, the library's holdings more than doubled, new services were introduced, and the branch system was extended.

Dudgeon's professional activities included serving as ALA treasurer from 1927 to 1941 and as president of the League of Library Commissions from 1914 to 1915.

DUNBAR, RALPH MCNEAL (1890-1970) was born in Elkton, Maryland, graduated from George Washington University in 1912, and received a master's degree from Columbia in 1914. He began his library career as an assistant in the District of Columbia Public Library from 1907 to 1912 and continued with various positions in the Brooklyn Public Library from 1913 to 1918. From 1919 through 1924, he was a field librarian with the morale division of the Bureau of Navigation, U.S. Navy. Afterward, he became assistant librarian at Iowa State College in Ames, associated with Charles H. Brown, and remained there until 1937. In 1937, he was appointed chief of the newly established library services division of the U.S. Office of Education. He was the first person to occupy that position and held wide-ranging responsibilities.

DUNKIN, PAUL SHANER (1905-1975) was born in Flora, Indiana, and graduated from DePauw University in 1929. He held two degrees from the University of Illinois, an M.A. in library science (1931) and a Ph.D. in classics (1937). He was a cataloger on the University of Illinois Library staff from 1935 to 1937. From

1937 to 1959, he was with the Folger Shakespeare Library in Washington, D.C., first as senior cataloger (1937-1950) and then as chief of technical services (1950-1959). From the Folger, he joined the faculty of the Graduate School of Library Service at Rutgers University, remaining there from 1959 to 1971.

Dunkin was known as an expert in the cataloging of rare books and played a key role in producing the *Anglo-American Cataloging Rules* (1967). He was president of the ALA resources and technical services division from 1964 to 1965 and editor of the journal *Library Resources and Technical Services.*

DUNLAP, LESLIE WHITTAKER (1911-   ) was born in Portland, Oregon, and graduated from the University of Oregon in 1933. He received three degrees from Columbia University — an A.M. in English (1938), a B.S. in library science (1942), and a Ph.D. in history. His professional positions have included reference and general assistant at the New York Public Library, 1936-1941; head of the acquisitions department at the University of Wisconsin Library, 1942-1945; assistant chief of the reference and bibliography division at the Library of Congress, 1945-1948; assistant chief of the manuscript division at the Library of Congress, 1948-1949; librarian at the University of British Columbia, 1949-1951; and associate director at the University of Illinois Library, Urbana, Illinois, 1951-1958. In 1958, he became director of the University of Iowa Libraries and held that position until his retirement in 1981.

Dunlap served as advisor to the National University of Mexico in 1948. He was president of the Iowa Library Association in 1968-1969 and a member of the first National Commission on Libraries and Information Service, appointed in 1970. Dunlap is the author of a number of books and journal articles, most recently *Our Vice Presidents and Their Ladies* (1988). Dunlap's doctoral studies in American history at Columbia University were directed by the eminent historian Allan Nevins.

EAMES, WILBERFORCE (1855-1937) was born in Newark, New Jersey, and became America's foremost bibliographer. In the Lenox Library (later consolidated with the New York Public Library), he was an assistant in 1885, an assistant librarian in 1892, and a librarian from 1893 to 1895. From its origin in 1909, he was librarian of the Bibliographical Society of America. Eames was author or editor of numerous works relating to the history of books and printing in America, including Sabin's *Dictionary of Books Relating to America.* He was awarded the London Bibliographical Society's gold medal in 1929.

EASTMAN, LINDA ANNE (1867-1963), who served the Cleveland Public Library for almost half a century, was born in Oberlin, Ohio, and attended the Cleveland Normal School. After teaching for six years, she worked in branch libraries of the Cleveland Public Library. In 1896, she became vice-librarian, second in command, of the entire Cleveland system. When William Brett was killed in 1918, Miss Eastman was the library board's unanimous choice to succeed him as head librarian. During her administration, the library expanded its services to hospitals, to the blind, and to municipal welfare institutions and established a travel section and a business information bureau. When Miss Eastman retired in 1938, the Cleveland Public Library had 1,200 employees and a book collection of more than two million volumes, while the library for the blind was serving about 30,000 registered readers.

In other professional activities, Miss Eastman was president of the Ohio Library Association from 1903 to 1904 and of the American Library Association from 1928 to 1929. She was a member of the faculty of the Western Reserve University Library School and received a variety of honorary degrees and special citations.

Eaton, Anne Thaxter (1881-1971), one of the great children's librarians, was born in Beverly Farms, Massachusetts. She graduated from Smith College and from the New York State Library School at Albany. Her first job was as librarian of the Pruyn Library in Albany from 1906 to 1910, after which she became assistant librarian of the University of Tennessee in Knoxville from 1910 to 1917. Returning to New York, she was appointed librarian of the new progressive school, Lincoln School of Columbia University's Teacher's College, where she served from 1917 until her retirement in 1946. She had a special talent for teaching students to love books and reading.

Miss Eaton was a regular reviewer for the *New York Times* from 1935 to 1946 and wrote hundreds of reviews for the *Times* and occasionally other journals. Her widely acclaimed books included *Reading with Children* (1956), *Treasure for the Taking* (1957), and a major anthology, *Animals' Christmas* (1944). Through her writing and reviewing, she influenced the tastes of children, parents, educators, and children's librarians for fifty years.

Edwards, Edward (1812-1886) was a major English librarian. He worked for the British Museum for eleven years and was chief librarian from 1850 to 1859 of the Manchester Public Library. He is regarded as the father of the public library movement in England and stimulated the formation of numerous public libraries throughout the country. During his stay at the British Museum, Edwards worked in the catalog department from 1839 to 1847 and helped to devise a new catalog code for the British Museum Library. From 1860 to 1864, he was employed in cataloging a private library, and he spent thirteen years, from 1870 to 1883, at Oxford University as a cataloger.

Edwards wrote numerous books dealing with libraries and English history. Among the best known are his *Free Town Libraries* (1869), *Libraries and Founders of Libraries* (1865), and *Memoirs of Libraries* (1859).

ELLSWORTH, RALPH EUGENE (1907-   ) was born on a farm near Forest City, Iowa. He graduated from Oberlin College and from the Western Reserve University Library School and holds a Ph.D. from the University of Chicago Graduate Library School. He began his half-century career as an academic librarian at Adams State College in Alamosa, Colorado, in 1931. Greater opportunities came in 1936, when Ellsworth became director of the University of Colorado Library at Boulder. In 1943, he was offered the library directorship at the University of Iowa. One of his first jobs at Iowa was to design a new library building, and there he pioneered the use of modular construction and flexible interior design. He also became well known as a consultant, especially in planning new buildings. In library association activities, Ellsworth served two terms (1951-1952 and 1960-1961) as president of the Association of College and Research Libraries, and in 1951, he was chairman of the ALA's 75th Anniversary Committee. He also took an active part in establishing the Council on Library Resources and the Center for Research Libraries.

After fourteen years at Iowa, Ellsworth returned to direct the University of Colorado libraries until his retirement in 1972. He is a prolific writer and has continued an extensive program of lecturing and consulting in the United States and in a number of foreign countries. Since 1940, he has been a building consultant in over 200 academic library projects, large and small. His published contributions in the field include *Planning Manual for Academic Library Buildings* and *Academic Library Buildings, A Guide to Architectural Issues and Solutions*, a companion piece published in 1973. He is also author of *The School Library: Facilities for Independent Study* (1968). His views as a political liberal are represented in a pamphlet, *The American Right Wing*, published in 1960.

Other areas in which Ellsworth has been deeply committed and influential are cooperative library cataloging, resource sharing, and the subject divisional plan for libraries. His autobiography,

Ellsworth on Ellsworth, was published in 1980 (Metuchen, N.J.: Scarecrow Press). Ellsworth was elected to honorary membership in the American Library Association in 1988.

ELMENDORF, THERESA (1855-1932) was born in Pardeeville, Wisconsin, and was educated in Milwaukee public schools. She stressed the benefits of public school and public library cooperation. An exceptional knowledge of books and confidence in the value of library service popularized her name and work in the professional world.

She was assistant librarian, and later librarian, in Milwaukee, Wisconsin, from 1892 to 1896 and founded the Wisconsin Library Association in 1897. From 1906 to 1926, she was vice-librarian at the Buffalo (New York) Public Library.

Elmendorf was editor for selection of the ALA's *Catalog for Small Libraries* (1904). She was president of the New York Library Association and the first woman president of American Library Association, serving from 1911 to 1912.

ESDAILE, ARUNDELL JAMES KENNEDY (1880-1956) was a native of London and a graduate of Magdalene College in Cambridge. He began in 1903 in the British Museum's department of printed books, and from 1926 to 1940, he was the museum's secretary. He lectured on bibliography in several institutions, edited the *Library Association Record* from 1923 to 1939, edited the *Year's Work in Librarianship* from 1929 to 1939, and was president of the Library Association from 1939 to 1945. He supported formation of the International Federation of Library Associations and paid a number of visits to the United States.

Esdaile was a prolific author. Among his works of permanent importance are *National Libraries of the World* (1934) and *The British Museum Library: A Short History* (1946).

ESHELMAN, WILLIAM ROBERT (1921-   ) was born in Oklahoma City, Oklahoma, and holds degrees from the University of California at Los Angeles and Berkeley. After a business career from 1941 to 1948, he became a library assistant at Berkeley, 1950-1951; assistant periodicals librarian at Los Angeles State College, 1951-1952; serials librarian, 1952-1953; assistant librarian, 1954-1959; and librarian, 1959-1965. From 1965 to 1968, he served as librarian and professor of bibliography at Bucknell University. Beginning in 1968, he became editor until 1978 of the *Wilson Library Bulletin*. He also has served as a consultant on library projects at Whittier College, at the University of Nevada, and at the University of West Florida. He has been a member of accreditation teams for various colleges and on numerous library association committees. He was president of the American Association of University Professors from 1964 to 1965 and editor of the *California Librarian* from 1960 to 1963. His specialties are planning academic library buildings, publishing for librarians, and academic library administration. He was president of Scarecrow Press from 1979 to 1986 and proprietor of the Press at the Camperdown Elm at Wooster, Ohio, in 1987.

ESTERQUEST, RALPH THEODORE (1912-1968) was born in Chicago, graduated from Northwestern University in 1933, and received two degrees in library science from the University of Illinois, in 1936 and 1940. His professional career was varied: he was a reference assistant and cataloger at Northwestern 1936-1937; an acquisitions assistant at the University of Illinois, 1938-1940; an assistant librarian of Princeton University's Institute of Advanced Study, 1940-1942; the manager of the ALA Publishing Department, 1942-1943; the director of the Pacific Northwest Bibliographic Center in Seattle, 1944-1946; an assistant director of the libraries at the University of Denver, 1946-1949; and the director of the Center for Research Libraries in Chicago, 1949-1958. In 1958, he became librarian of the Harvard Medical School. In 1965, Esterquest was appointed librarian of the Francis A. Countway Library of Medicine at Harvard University, where he remained until his death in 1968.

In 1953-1954, Esterquest studied library cooperation in the British Isles under a Fulbright Fellowship and in 1967-1968 was director of the ALA International Relations office.

Esterquest was the leader in establishing the Mountain-Plains Library Association and served as its first president in 1948. He was also president of the Chicago Library Club and was an active member of the American Library Association and the Illinois Library Association. His primary interests were interlibrary cooperation and medical librarianship.

EVANS, CHARLES (1850-1935) was an assistant in the Boston Athenaeum when he conceived his monumental project of listing the approximately 50,000 American imprints from 1639 to 1820. By the time of his death, he had verified about 36,000 of the total, to 1799. The record was published in twelve quarto volumes under the title of *American Bibliography, a Chronological Dictionary of All Books, Pamphlets and Periodical Publications Printed in the United States of America from the Genesis of Printing in 1639 Down to and Including 1820*. A supplement, sponsored by the Bibliographical Society of America, completed the record to 1820.

Evans was one of the founders of the American Library Association. He was librarian of the Indianapolis Public Library from 1872 to 1880 and of the Enoch Pratt Library in Baltimore from 1884 to 1887. He also reorganized the Omaha Public Library, classified the Newberry Library (1892-1895), and was executive secretary and librarian of the Chicago Historical Society (1896-1901).

EVANS, LUTHER HARRIS (1902-1981) was born in Sayersville, Texas. He received A.B. and A.M. degrees in political science from the University of Texas (1923-1924) and a Ph.D. degree from Stanford University (1927). He gained teaching experience at Texas, Stanford, New York University, Dartmouth, and Princeton and spent two years in Europe studying the governments of England, France, and Switzerland and the activities of the League of Nations.

In 1935, Evans became director of the WPA's Historical Records Survey. Under his guidance, a nationwide inventory of historical source materials led to the publication of several hundred guides. The next step for Evans was appointment as director of the legislative reference service of the Library of Congress in 1939. The following year, he was promoted to chief assistant librarian, and in June 1945, he was appointed librarian of Congress by President Harry Truman. An enormous increase occurred in the library's acquisitions during Evans's administration, and he worked assiduously to make the institution a truly national library, not simply the Library of Congress. Deeply concerned with international affairs, in 1953, Evans resigned as librarian of Congress to become the third director general of UNESCO from 1953 to 1958. From 1962 to 1971, Evans served as director of the international and legal collections at Columbia University.

FAIRCHILD, MARY SALOME CUTLER (1855-1921) was a graduate of Bryn Mawr College. She was employed by Melvil Dewey as head of the catalog department of Columbia College and then as an instructor in cataloging. She followed Dewey to Albany as vice-director of the New York State Library School. For the next fifteen years, she was chief administrator in all but name of the school. She combined her teaching duties with serving as librarian of the New York State Library for the Blind at Albany. She was chairman of an ALA committee to assemble a model library for the 1893 Columbia Exposition in Chicago, the catalog of which was published by the U.S. Federal Bureau of Education.

FARGO, LUCILLE FOSTER (1880-1962) was born in Lake Mills, Wisconsin. She earned two degrees from Whitman College (1903-1904) and a certificate from the New York State Library School at Albany. After appointments on the Portland (Oregon) Public Library staff, she was librarian at North Central High School in Spokane, Washington, from 1909 to 1926. In 1926, she became general assistant for the ALA board of education for a year and there wrote a text in its field, *The Library in the School* (1928). She went on to the field of library education at the Columbia School of Library Service from 1933 to 1935, at the George Peabody Library School from 1930 to 1933, and at the Western Reserve School of Library Science from 1937 to 1945. She retired in 1945 to devote full time to writing. She is regarded as a pioneer in the school library field.

FAXON, FREDERICK WINTHROP (1866-1936) was born at West Roxbury, Massachusetts, and graduated from Harvard in 1889. He was not a professional librarian, but his publishing activities, in particular, were of valuable assistance to library service. In 1897, he established the *Bulletin of Bibliography*; in 1908, the *Annual Magazine Subject Index*; and, in 1909, the *Dramatic Index*.

Faxon was secretary of the American Library Association from 1900 to 1903 and president of the Massachusetts Library Club from 1931 to 1932. In 1912, he was an official ALA delegate to the meeting of the Library Association of Great Britain at Liverpool. He was a veteran traveler, visiting all states in the United States and numerous European countries.

FELLOWS, JENNE DORCAS (1873-1938) was born in Griswold, Connecticut. She received a diploma from the New York State Library School and went to work for Melvil Dewey at the New York State Library. She prepared a text on *Cataloging Rules* (1914) that is used widely in libraries and library schools. New editions of the Dewey classification were edited by her from 1921 until her death.

FENSTER, VALMAI KIRKHAM (1939-1984) was a native of New Zealand and held degrees from the University of New Zealand. Her first library degree was from the University of Illinois, followed by a doctorate from the University of Wisconsin. For fifteen years she was on the faculty of the University of Wisconsin Library School. She was author of a standard reference work, *Guide to American Literature* (1983), established a scholarship to help foreign students come to the United States to study librarianship, and was chairman of the ALA international relations round table.

FERGUSON, MILTON JAMES (1879-1954) was born in Hubbardstown, West Virginia. He attended the University of Oklahoma from 1901 to 1906, graduating with A.B. and A.M. degrees. He received a certificate in librarianship from New York State University in Albany in 1902. He returned to Oklahoma to serve as librarian of the University of Oklahoma from 1902 to 1907. He next moved to California to become assistant state librarian in charge of the law collection, from 1908 to 1917, and afterward became state librarian until 1930. During 1928 to 1929, Ferguson undertook library surveys for the Carnegie Corporation in the Union of South Africa, Rhodesia, and Kenya Colony.

In 1930, Ferguson was appointed chief librarian of the Brooklyn (New York) Public Library, where he remained until reaching retirement in 1949. His accomplishments at Brooklyn included opening the central library, developing a regional branch system, organizing a business reference branch, and working on staff reforms. He was president of the American Library Association from 1938 to 1939 and was also president of the California and New York library associations, as well as of the National Association of State Libraries.

FLETCHER, WILLIAM ISAAC (1844-1917) was born in Burlington, Vermont, although he grew up in Boston. He was introduced to library work by serving as librarian of the small town library in Winchester. From 1861 to 1866, he was on the staff of the Boston Athenaeum, in charge of the circulation desk. After leaving the athenaeum in 1866, Fletcher served as librarian in Lawrence and Taunton, Massachusetts, and in Waterbury, Connecticut, all of which had newly established libraries in urban industrial centers. That period was followed by a term as assistant librarian in the Watkinson Library at Hartford, Connecticut. In 1883, Fletcher was appointed librarian at Amherst College and retired in 1911. In 1891, Fletcher began his summer school for librarians, which attracted students from other states; it had an enrollment of fifty-four in 1902.

In 1882, Fletcher became associate editor of *Poole's Index to Periodical Literature*, and after William Poole's death in 1894, Fletcher served as editor starting with the 1893 supplement. Fletcher also edited the *ALA Index to General Literature* from 1893 to 1901, indexing the contents of books. From 1893 to 1910, Fletcher and his associate, Helen E. Haines, edited the *Annual Library Index*.

Fletcher was a leader in the American Library Association and succeeded Samuel Swett Green as ALA president for the 1891-1892 term.

FLEXNER, JENNIE MAAS (1882-1944) was born in Louisville, Kentucky. She was related to Abraham Flexner, noted for his works on medical education and higher education, and to Simon Flexner, an eminent bacteriologist. Her career in librarianship began in 1905 in the Louisville Public Library. In 1909, she received a certificate from the Western Reserve University Library School. Back in Louisville, she was placed in charge of the library's training class, and in 1912, she was appointed head of the circulation department. From 1923 to 1925, she was president of the Kentucky Library Association. In 1928, she was chosen to establish a readers' advisory service for the New York Public Library. She provided professional leadership toward meeting some of the basic social problems of the time for foreign-born refugees and for young men and women in military service during World War II. Her early death in 1944 ended Miss Flexner's brilliant career. She contributed two important books, *Circulation Work in Public Libraries* (1927) and *Making Books Work* (1943). She was second vice-president of the American Library Association (1929-1930).

FOSTER, WILLIAM EATON (1851-1930) was a native of Vermont and a graduate of Brown University. His first position as a librarian was at the Hyde Park (Massachusetts) Library from 1873 to 1876, followed by part-time employment at the Boston Public Library. In 1878, he was appointed librarian of the Providence (Rhode Island) Public Library. Under Foster's strong management, the library erected a new central building and established a children's department along with art and music divisions. Twelve branches of the library were created, and there were large increases in the size of the book collection and in circulation.

Foster was one of the founding members of the American Library Association in 1876.

FRANCIS, FRANK CHALTON (1901-1988) was one of the most famous of modern English librarians. He was a former director and principal librarian of the British Museum. He was educated at Liverpool and Cambridge universities and began his career as a schoolmaster. His connection with the British Museum started in 1926. Later he became secretary (1946-1947), keeper in the department of printed books, and director (1958-1968). He had a particular interest in historical bibliography, a field in which he was active in writing and editing. For many years he lectured at the School of Librarianship at University College in London. He served as president of the Library Association, the Bibliographical Society, the Association of Special Libraries and Information Bureau, the Museums Association, and the International Federation of Library Associations. He edited *The Library* for eighteen years and *The Journal of Documentation* for twenty-two years. He was instrumental in founding the *British National Bibliography* and in publishing the third edition of the British Museum's *General Catalogue of Printed Books*. Sir Francis was knighted in 1960.

FRANKLIN, BENJAMIN (1706-1790) — statesman, scientist, printer, publisher, writer, and librarian — was born in Boston, although much of his career was spent in Philadelphia. In 1731, at the age of twenty-five, Franklin and a group of like-minded young men, about fifty in number, established the Philadelphia Library Company, a subscription library that was the first to be founded in the United States. This was the predecessor of lending libraries that were dependent on voluntary contributions. They were called, variously, association libraries, mechanics' and apprentices' libraries, and mercantile libraries. The collection included many subjects, and the books were ordered mainly from England. Franklin was the first librarian. The Library Company has continued to flourish to the present day. Franklin was active in starting the American Philosophical Society Library in 1749 and served as its secretary. The society exchanged its publications with a number of foreign societies. Franklin contributed also to the Harvard and Yale university libraries.

FRANTZ, RAY WILLIAM, JR. (1923-   ) was born in Princeton, Kentucky. He graduated from the University of Nebraska in 1948 and from the University of Illinois Library School in 1951. In 1955, he earned a Ph.D. in English at the University of Illinois. From 1955 to 1960, he was director of the University of Richmond Library, and from 1960 to 1962, he was associate director of the Ohio State University Library. He became director of libraries at the University of Wyoming in 1962 and held that position until 1967, when he became librarian at the University of Virginia. Frantz served with the U.S. Army in World War II from 1943 to 1946. He was president of the Association of Research Libraries, 1977-1978; chairman of the board of directors of Solinet, 1975-

1976; and chairman of the Association of Southeastern Research Libraries, 1975-1977.

FREEHAFER, EDWARD GRIER (1909-1985) had a library career of thirty-eight years, almost entirely with the New York Public Library. He was born in Reading, Pennsylvania, and graduated from Brown University in 1930. In 1932, he graduated from the Columbia School of Library Service. He began as an assistant in the New York Public Library main reading room, then became chief of the American history and genealogy division from 1941 to 1942. From 1942 to 1944, he was acting chief of the acquisition division, and in 1954, he became chief of the reference department. From 1954 to 1971, he was the sixth director of the New York Public Library, the youngest director in the library's history. The only break was a year spent at Brown University as assistant librarian, 1944-1945. During his term as director, Freehafer established the Research Library of the Performing Arts at Lincoln Center.

FUSSLER, HERMAN HOWE (1914-   ) was born in Philadelphia and graduated from the University of North Carolina. He holds M.A. and Ph.D. degrees from the University of Chicago in library science. In 1936, he was an assistant in the New York Public Library's science and technology division. At the University of Chicago Library, he began as head of the department of photoreproduction (1936-1946), during which he spent two years in France. From 1943 to 1947, he served as science librarian, and in 1947, he became assistant director. This was followed by his appointment as associate director, from 1947 to 1948, and as director, from 1948 to 1971. He was also on the faculty of the Graduate Library School at Chicago, starting in 1942, and served as acting dean from 1961 to 1963. He was a consultant for the Ford Foundation at the University of Sao Paulo, Brazil, in 1962, and a visiting professor at the University of Monash in Australia in 1977. Fussler was presented with the ALA Melvil Dewey Medal in 1954. He is recognized as an authority on photographic reproduction for libraries and is the author of books relating to that subject, to library buildings, and to the use of books in research libraries. Since 1949, he has been associate editor of the *Library Quarterly*.

GALVIN, HOYT REESE (1912-   ) was born in Pleasantville, Iowa. He graduated from Simpson College and from the University of Illinois Library School in 1932. He was director of the Charlotte and Mecklenburg County (North Carolina) Public Library from 1941 to 1971 and developed it into one of the outstanding public libraries in the South. He has served as a building consultant for over 200 libraries and since 1954 has headed his own consulting organization, Hoyt Galvin and Associates. He has served as president of four state, regional, and national library associations. Simpson College conferred its Alumni Achievement Award on him in 1970, and he received the Southeastern Library Association's Outstanding Public Library Award.

GARNETT, RICHARD (1835-1906) has been called "the most significant figure in the British Museum's history since Panizzi." In 1851, at sixteen years of age, he was employed at the British Museum. Later he became assistant keeper of books and superintendent of the reading room. Garnett was deeply interested in cataloging, and he proposed that the library's numerous manuscript catalogs be replaced with a printed catalog. This catalog, which recorded all holdings up to 1900, was completed in 1905, twenty-four years later. Garnett was promoted to the post of keeper of printed books. He retired in 1899, after which he became a prolific writer on biography and literature. He authored a pioneer work, *Essays in Librarianship and Bibliography* (1899).

GAVER, MARY VIRGINIA (1906-   ) was born in Washington, D.C., and graduated from Randolph-Macon College in Lynchburg, Virginia, in 1927. She later earned two degrees, in 1932 and 1938, from the Columbia School of Library Service. Her first library experience was as an apprentice in the District of Columbia Public Library. In 1938-1939, she was employed as technical director of a statewide WPA library project in Virginia, and from 1939 to 1942, she was a high school librarian in Scarsdale, New York. She was also active as a teacher of library science at the University of Virginia from 1933 to 1938, at Emory University from 1939 to 1942, at New Jersey State Teacher's College at Trenton from 1942 to 1954, and at the University of Teheran for the International Information Administration from 1952 to 1953. In 1952, she joined the faculty of the Graduate School of Library Service at Rutgers University, retiring in 1971.

Miss Gaver was president of the New Jersey Library Association, 1954-1955; president of the ALA library education division, 1949-1950; and president of the American Library Association, 1966-1967. The Herbert Putnam Honor Award was presented to her in 1963 in recognition of her "significant contributions to the profession of librarianship,"

GEROULD, JAMES THAYER (1872-1951) was born in Goffstown, New Hampshire, and graduated from Dartmouth College in 1895. He held a number of library administrative positions: he was assistant librarian of the General Theological Seminary, 1896-1897; chief of a Columbia University library department, 1897-1900; librarian of the University of Missouri, 1900-1906; librarian of the University of Minnesota, 1906-1920; and finally, librarian of Princeton University, 1920-1938. He held editorial posts with *The Bellman* (1916-1918) and *Current History Magazine*

(1926-1933). His books and articles include the *College Library Building* (1932). His second wife was Winifred Gregory, editor of the *Union List of Serials in Libraries of the United States and Canada* (1927 and 1943) and of other major bibliographical compilations.

GEROULD, WINIFRED GREGORY (1885-1955) held several library positions: she worked for the University of Minnesota loan department, was librarian of the Riverside branch of the Minneapolis Public Library, was chief of the industrial arts department at the St. Paul Public Library (1917-1920), and worked in the Carnegie Library of Pittsburgh's technology division. She is best known as a bibliographer who served as editor of the *Union List of Serials in Libraries of the United States and Canada, Serials of Foreign Governments, American Newspapers, 1821-1936*, and *International Congresses and Conferences, 1840-1937*. She was married in 1940 to James Thayer Gerould, a retired Princeton University librarian.

GILCHRIST, DONALD BEAN (1892-1939) was born in Franklin, New Hampshire. He graduated from Dartmouth in 1913 and from the New York State Library School in 1915. He spent a year with the interlibrary loan department of the University of Minnesota and then was in military service in Mexico and France from 1916 to 1918. After returning to civilian life, he was appointed, in 1919, as librarian of the University of Rochester, where he remained until his sudden death in 1939.

Gilchrist was one of the organizers of the Association of Research Libraries, for which he was executive secretary from 1932 to 1937. He was the first editor of the annual *Doctoral Dissertations Accepted by American Universities* (1933-1939).

GILLETT, CHARLES RIPLEY (1855-1948) was born in New York City, graduated in civil engineering from New York University, and studied for two years (1881-1883) at the University of Berlin. Gillett became librarian of Union Theological Seminary in

1883 and remained in that position until 1908 as head of the largest theological seminary library in the United States. Previously, his appointments as a student assistant and part-time staff member had continued for twenty-three years, making a total of sixty-nine years in one institution. Professionally, he developed an important scheme of classification for a theological collection and compiled a number of major bibliographical works, including a five-volume catalogue of the *McAlpin Collection of British History and Theology*.

GILLIS, JAMES LOUIS (1857-1917), California state librarian for eighteen years, was born in Richmond, Iowa. After he became director of the state library in 1899, he instituted a number of basic reforms: traveling libraries, legislative reference service, active promotion of county libraries, regional branches, a library school in the state library, and a new building for the crowded library. By the time of Gillis's death in 1917, all except twenty-two of California's counties had complete library service.

Gillis was president of the California Library Association for eight terms, from 1906 to 1915, and president of the National Association of State Librarians in 1906 and 1914.

GILLIS, MABEL RAY (1882-1961) was born in Sacramento, California, the daughter of the California state librarian. She graduated from the University of California and began her library career at the California State Library's department serving the blind. She continued as assistant to Milton J. Ferguson, state librarian, and finally was appointed to be the eleventh state librarian of California, the first woman to hold that position. During World War II, she was the California director of the Victory Book Campaign. She retired in 1951 after forty-seven years on the California State Library staff.

In 1928-1929, Miss Gillis served as president of the California Library Association and in 1934-1935 as president of the National Association of State Libraries.

GILMAN, DANIEL COIT (1831-1908) was born in Norwich, Connecticut, and graduated from Yale in 1852. Over the next six decades, he was librarian of Yale College, 1856-1865; professor at the Sheffield Scientific School of Yale, 1863-1872; president of the University of California, 1872-1875; president of Johns Hopkins University, 1875-1901; and president of the Carnegie Institution of Washington, 1902-1904.

When Gilman took over its direction in 1856, the Yale library was rated the largest academic library in the country. Lack of financial support by President Theodore Dwight Woolsey caused a gradual loss of its high rank, leading Gilman to resign in 1865 as a protest.

While president of Johns Hopkins University, Gilman actively promoted library cooperation by depending on the resources of the Peabody Institute and other Baltimore libraries, encouraging interlibrary loans and publishing the nation's first regional union list of current periodicals. By 1900, the Johns Hopkins Library was rated the tenth largest academic library.

Gilman's interest in libraries continued. He served as vice-president of the American Library Association from 1882 to 1883 and was a member of the ALA Council from 1883 to 1886. He was also a trustee on the governing boards of the Peabody and Enoch Pratt libraries.

GJELSNESS, RUDOLPH H. (1894-1968) was born in Reynolds, North Dakota, and graduated from the University of North Dakota in 1912. After military service in World War I, he joined the University of Illinois Library staff and completed a B.L.S. degree in 1920. In 1920-1922, he was order librarian at the University of Oregon, followed by the position of senior bibliographer at the University of California. The year 1924-1925 was spent at the University of Oslo. His long association with the University of Michigan started in 1925 when he was appointed assistant librarian and chief classifier. For three years (1929-1932), he was chief of the preparation division of the New York Public Library, and from 1932 to 1937 he was head librarian of the University of Arizona.

In 1937, Gjelsness returned to Michigan as a professor of library science and in 1940 succeeded William Warner Bishop as chairman of the department of library science, where he remained until his retirement in 1965. He was strongly committed to international librarianship. In 1942, he directed a summer school at Bogota, Colombia, and in 1943-1944, he was director of the Benjamin Franklin Library in Mexico City. He served as consultant to the president of the University of Baghdad in Iraq from 1962 to 1963.

After his retirement at Michigan, Gjelsness returned to the University of Arizona as head of the library's special collections division from 1965 until his accidental death in 1968.

GOGGIN, MARGARET KNOX (1919-) was born in Nyack, New York. She graduated from Maryville College in 1940 and from the Peabody Library School in 1942. She holds master's and doctoral degrees (1948 and 1957) from the University of Illinois Library School. She was a teacher-librarian at Flintwood (Tennessee) High School from 1940 to 1942, a reference assistant at the Joint University Library in Nashville, Tennessee, from 1942 to 1943, acting reference librarian from 1943 to 1945, a visiting instructor at the Peabody Library School from 1943 to 1945, a bibliographer and reference librarian at the Office of Technical Services at the Department of Commerce in Washington, D.C. from 1946 to 1947, a reference assistant at the University of Illinois from 1948 to 1949, assistant to the director at the University of Florida libraries from 1949 to 1950, head of the reference and bibliography divisions at the University of Florida from 1950 to 1962, and acting director of the University of Florida libraries from 1967 to 1968.

In 1968, Mrs. Goggin was appointed dean of the University of Denver Graduate School of Librarianship. There she carried on many of the traditions and practices of the first Denver director,

Harriet E. Howe. She has been an active member of the American Library Association and has carried out missions to Haiti and Paris as a representative of the Rockefeller Foundation. In 1968-1969, she was president of the ALA reference services division.

GOLDHOR, HERBERT (1917-   ), prominent library educator, was born in Newark, New Jersey, and graduated from Dana College in 1935. In 1938, he graduated from the Columbia School of Library Service, and he received his Ph.D. degree from the Graduate Library School at the University of Chicago in 1942. He was an assistant at the Newark Public Library from 1933 to 1937 and assistant to the librarian of Iowa State College at Ames from 1938 to 1939. At the University of Illinois, he was first assistant professor and then associate professor from 1946 to 1952. He became associate director of the Graduate School of Library Science in 1962 and director in 1963. He held that position until 1978. From 1975 to 1987, he was also director of the Library Research Center at the University of Illinois. From 1952 to 1961, Goldhor served as chief librarian at the Evansville (Indiana) Public Library. He is coauthor with Joseph L. Wheeler of *Practical Administration of Public Libraries*. During World War II, he served as a lieutenant in the U.S. Army from 1944 to 1946.

The ALA presented Goldhor with the Melvil Dewey Medal in 1988.

GOODRICH, FRANCIS LEE DEWEY (1877-1962) was born in Manchester, Michigan. He graduated in 1903 from the University of Michigan and from the New York State Library School in 1906. He also held a master's degree in medieval history from Michigan (1916). His first library experience was as assistant librarian of Eastern Michigan University from 1900 to 1904. He worked briefly at the John Crerar Library, and from 1907 to 1930, he held various positions at the University of Michigan. For fifteen years (1930-1945), he headed the City College of New York Library, where he developed a substantially increased collection, tripled circulation, and nearly doubled the staff. After retiring from CCNY in 1945, Goodrich joined the staff of the Clements Library at the University of Michigan in 1945 until his death in 1962 at age eighty-five.

Goodrich was editor of *Michigan Libraries* (1910-1914) and coauthor with William Randall of a well-known textbook, *Principles of College Library Administration* (1936).

GORMAN, MICHAEL (1941-   ) was born in Oxfordshire, England. He was head of cataloging for the British National Bibliography from 1969 to 1972. He became director of the technical services department at the University of Illinois Library in 1977 and remained in that position until he was appointed director of the California State College Library at Fresno in 1988. He received the Margaret Mann Citation from the American Library Association's resources and technical services division in 1975. He is the author of *AACR2* (1981), the joint edition, and of the second edition of *Anglo-American Cataloging Rules* (1978). He became a fellow of the British Library Association in 1978.

GOVAN, JAMES FAUNTLEROY (1926-   ) is a native of Chattanooga, Tennessee. He graduated from the University of the South in 1948 and did postgraduate work at the Institute for Historical Research at the University of London from 1951 to 1952. In 1955, he earned an M.A. from Emory University, and in 1960, he received a Ph.D. in history from Johns Hopkins University. His professional career began as readers services librarian at the University of Alabama (1955-1960), as head librarian of Trinity University (1961-1965), and as librarian of Swarthmore College (1965-1973). Since 1973, Govan has been university librarian at the University of North Carolina at Chapel Hill. Govan served with the U.S. Naval Reserve from 1944 to 1946 and with the U.S. Army from 1953 to 1955. In 1981-1982, he was president of the Association of Research Libraries.

GRAHAM, CLARENCE (1907-) was born in Louisville, Kentucky, and was a student at the University of North Carolina from 1924 to 1927. He graduated from the University of Louisville in 1934 and from the Western Reserve Library School in 1935. He began his library career as librarian of Parkland Junior High School in Louisville from 1930 to 1934. From 1935 to 1936, he was assistant to the librarian of the Louisville Public Library, and from 1936 to 1942, he was director of the National College of Education Library. In 1942, he became director of the Louisville Public Library.

Graham was president of the Kentucky Library Association (1946-1947), president of the Southeastern Library Association (1948-1950), and president of the American Library Association (1950-1951).

The Louisville Public Library, under Graham's direction, was a pioneer in the use of radio for library purposes. It was the first library to receive a broadcasting permit by the Federal Communications Commission for educational and cultural programs.

GREEN, SAMUEL SWETT (1837-1918) was born in Worcester, Massachusetts, and graduated from Harvard in 1858. In 1871, after a period of serving as a trustee, he became librarian of the Worcester Public Library, a position in which he remained until his resignation in 1909. The library flourished under his guidance; new branches and a children's department were organized.

Green was active in national and international librarianship. He presided over the World Congress of Librarians held in Chicago in 1893. He was one of the leaders in the first American Library Association conference in Philadelphia, in 1876, and was ALA president in 1891.

GREENAWAY, EMERSON (1906-) was born in Springfield, Massachusetts, and graduated from the University of Massachusetts in 1927. He earned a degree in library science from the University of North Carolina in 1935. Greenaway held a variety of positions: he was an assistant in the reference room of Springfield's City Library Association in 1928; he was supervisor of branches and assistant librarian of the Hartford (Connecticut) Public Library from 1930 to 1934; he was librarian of the Fitchburg (Massachusetts) Public Library from 1937 to 1940; he served as librarian of the Worcester (Massachusetts) Public Library from 1940 to 1945; he was director of the Enoch Pratt Library in Baltimore from 1945 to 1951; and he served as director of the Philadelphia Free Library from 1951 to 1969. For UNESCO, he made a survey of library conditions in Czechoslovakia, Austria, and Poland in 1947. He was a member of the United States delegation of librarians to the U.S.S.R. in 1961.

Greenaway was vice-president of the American Library Association from 1945 to 1946 and ALA president from 1958 to 1959. He was awarded the Lippincott Award by the ALA in 1955.

GREENE, BELLE DA COSTA (1883-1950) was born in Alexandria, Virginia. After a brief apprenticeship in the Princeton University Library under Ernest C. Richardson, she was chosen by Pierpont Morgan as librarian in charge of his private collection. In 1924, the Pierpont Morgan Library was incorporated as a public institution. For the next twenty-four years, until her retirement in 1948, Miss Greene remained as director. During that period, the Morgan Library became world-famous for its rare book collections: illuminated manuscripts, incunabula, fine bindings, and other rarities.

GREENWOOD, THOMAS (1851-1908), born in the English north country, has been described as the apostle of the English library movement. His association with books began when he was a traveling salesman. In 1874, he became assistant librarian at the Sheffield Public Library. Later, as a magazine publisher, he was an active promoter of public libraries. Toward that purpose, he published in 1886 an influential book, *Free Public Libraries*, which went through a number of editions. He financed the publication of Duff Brown's *Manual of Library Economy* (1900) and Edward Edwards's *Memoirs of Libraries* (1902). In 1901, Greenwood was elected honorary fellow of the Library Association.

Gregorian, Vartan (1934-   ) was born to an American family in Tabriz, Iran. After a distinguished career as dean and provost of the University of Pennsylvania (1974-1980), he was appointed president of the New York Public Library in 1981. There he faced a multitude of problems: a physical plant in decay, a demoralized staff, and a serious shortage of money. The great library had fallen on hard times since it had been created eighty-six years earlier by the merger of the John Jacob Astor and James Lenox private libraries with funds from the Tilden trust. Over a period of seven years, Gregorian achieved an amazing transformation by curing the library's physical and financial problems and restoring it to the center of New York's cultural life. He resigned in 1988 to become president of Brown University.

During the Gregorian regime, the NYPL operating budget went from $60 million to $118 million, the endowment increased from $94 million to $150 million, and the landmark building at Fifth Avenue and Forty-Second Street was restored. Gregorian remains as a trustee and vice-chairman of the NYPL board.

Griffin, Appleton Prentiss Clark (1852-1926) was born in Wilson, New Hampshire. His sixty-year career as a librarian was spent in four libraries: the Boston Public Library, the Boston Athenaeum, the Lenox Library in New York, and the Library of Congress. From 1865 to 1894, he was associated with the Boston Public Library, beginning as a "runner" or messenger boy. It was here that he gained the reputation of being one of the best bibliographers in the country. For the athenaeum he prepared a catalog of its Washington collection (1897). His appointment to the Library of Congress staff began in 1897 and continued for the remainder of his career, progressing from chief bibliographer to chief assistant librarian, in 1908. He became the chief reference librarian of the Library of Congress and the library's chief advisor on book selection.

GRIGGS, LILLIAN BAKER (1876-1955) was born in Anderson, South Carolina, and graduated from Agnes Scott College. Her career was divided between public and college libraries. After receiving a library certificate from Emory University in 1911, she was appointed director of the Durham (North Carolina) Public Library. The library's management with volunteer workers had been haphazard, but under Mrs. Griggs, the entire collection was classified and cataloged, the appropriation was doubled, a children's room with story hours was initiated, and a Carnegie grant was obtained for a new library building. A branch library was set up in Durham's mill district, a library was organized at the city's high school, books were circulated to county schools, a library for blacks was begun, and a library in the local hospital was provided. A bookmobile, the first in North Carolina, expanded service to rural areas. In cooperation with Louis R. Wilson at the University of North Carolina, Mrs. Griggs helped to organize the citizens' library movement to fight for countywide library service throughout the state. During World War I, Mrs. Griggs was deeply committed to providing library service to the armed forces. In 1919, she was stationed with the army of occupation in Germany.

Library association activities were a major concern for Mrs. Griggs. She was president of the North Carolina Association in 1917-1918 and in 1931, director of the North Carolina Library Commission in 1923, and president of the National League of Library Commissions. Years later, she became president of the Southeastern Library Association (1932-1933).

A new phase of Mrs. Griggs's career began in 1930 when she was appointed librarian of Duke University's new women's college. She developed the book collection, provided a browsing room, added books important for women's education, inspired Duke to offer a course in children's literature for which the library supplied books, and began the then revolutionary plan of open stacks for students. A biographer notes that long after her retirement, following nineteen years as the director, "the Woman's College Library at Duke University continued to reflect the dynamic personality and expertise of Lillian Griggs."

Hadley, Chalmers (1872-1958) was born in Indianapolis. He graduated from Earlham College in 1896 and from the New York State Library School in 1906. In 1906, he was appointed secretary and state organizer of the Indiana Library Commission. Three years later, he became executive secretary of the American Library Association, a position that he held until 1911. Two major administrative jobs followed: he was director of the Denver Public Library from 1911 to 1924 and director of the Cincinnati Public Library from 1924 to 1926.

Hadley participated in professional organizations as president of the League of Library Commissioners (1907-1908), president of the Colorado Library Association (1914), president of the American Library Association (1919-1920), president of the Ohio Library Association (1925), and president of the Ohio Historical and Philosophical Society (1945). During World War I, he served actively with various war library programs.

Haines, Helen Elizabeth (1872-1961) was preeminent as a book reviewer. She edited the third supplement of the *American Catalog* (1890-1895) and the *Annual Library Index* (1905-1910). She also taught classes dealing with acquisition work in library schools. Her best-known work was *Living with Books; The Art of Book Selection* (1950), which demonstrated intimate knowledge of books in a variety of subjects. Miss Haines was also managing editor of the *Library Journal* from 1895 to 1908.

HANSON, JAMES CHRISTIAN MEINICH (1864-1943) has been called "one of the three or four librarians whose work has had the greatest effect on the appearance of the catalogs in use in American libraries today." His major contributions were twofold: the form and content of the Library of Congress printed card, and the *Catalog Rules* issued by the American and British library associations in 1908.

Hanson was born in Norway but came to the United States at age nine. He graduated from Luther College in Iowa and from Concordia Seminary in St.Louis and was a graduate student at Cornell University. In 1890, he began a three-year stay at the newly organized Newberry Library in Chicago, working under William Frederick Poole. In 1893, he became head of the catalog department at the University of Wisconsin. Four years later, Hanson was appointed chief of the Library of Congress cataloging division. With the assistance of Charles Martel, a new classification system was developed to replace the outmoded scheme devised by Thomas Jefferson. Under Hanson, the Library of Congress became the first American library to print its cards, including fifty copies of each card to exchange with or sell to other libraries. An international agreement on cataloging methods was reached between the American and British library associations, leading to the adoption of the 1908 code.

Hanson left the Library of Congress in 1910 to become associate director and to take charge of cataloging for the University of Chicago. In 1928, he joined the faculty of the university's new Graduate Library School and remained there until his retirement in 1934, with time out to advise the Vatican Library on recataloging its collections, to teach at Columbia and Michigan, and to serve as a consultant at the Library of Congress.

HAZELTINE, MARY IMOGENE (1868-1949) graduated from Wellesley College in 1891. After a period as librarian of the Prendergast Free Library (1893-1906), she was appointed head of the

University of Wisconsin School of Library Science, where her organizing genius was demonstrated from 1906 to 1938, when she retired. She served as president of the New York Library Association in 1902.

Miss Hazeltine was the author of a standard reference work, *Anniversaries and Holidays* (1928 and later editions).

HEWINS, CAROLINE MARIA (1846-1926) was born in Roxbury, Massachusetts. She became librarian of the Young Men's Institute of Hartford, Connecticut, an institution that developed into the city's public library in 1892. Miss Hewins remained here for fifty years until her death at age eighty. In a variety of ways, she stimulated library service for children and children's reading interests. In 1904, she opened a children's library in a building adjacent to the main library.

In 1891, Miss Hewins helped to found the Connecticut Library Association and later served as its president. She was appointed secretary of the Connecticut Public Library Commission in 1893, and vice-president of the American Library Association in 1891, and she actively promoted formation of a children's librarians section. The Caroline M. Hewins scholarship for young women librarians was established in 1926.

HILL, FRANK PIERCE (1855-1941) was born in Concord, New Hampshire, and graduated from Dartmouth College in 1876. He soon established a reputation as an organizer of public libraries, including those in Lowell, Massachusetts (1879-1884), Paterson, New Jersey (1885-1887), and Salem, Massachusetts (1888). He became the first librarian of the Newark (New Jersey) Public Library in 1889 and remained in that position until 1901. One of his principal achievements at Newark was the erection of a new library building.

In 1901, Hill began a thirty-year tenure as chief librarian of the Brooklyn Public Library, during which the library's collections grew from 360,000 to 1,035,000 volumes and circulation increased from 1,614,000 to 7,838,000.

Hill actively participated in the American Library Association's affairs: he was secretary, succeeding Melvil Dewey, from 1891 to 1895, vice-president in 1904, and president from 1905 to 1906. He attended the International Exhibit of Book Industries at Leipzig in 1914.

HIRSHBERG, HERBERT SIMON (1879-1955) was born in Boston and graduated from Harvard in 1900. He attended a "summer school of library economy" taught by William I. Fletcher at Amherst and then became a cataloger of foreign books in the Boston Public Library. He earned a B.L.S. degree from the New York State Library School at Albany (1903-1905) and at the same time was employed as a cataloger in the New York State Library. His next position was as a music cataloger at the Library of Congress. In 1908, William Brett appointed Hirshberg as a reference librarian at the Cleveland Public Library. While holding that post, he was an instructor at the Western Reserve Library School and directed the establishment of a municipal reference branch for the city government.

In 1914, Hirshberg left Cleveland to become director of the Toledo Public Library and there helped to establish an extensive branch library system. The next move occurred in 1922, when he became Ohio state librarian. He initiated important reforms in the Ohio library world until 1927, when the state library was closed because of the governor's veto of its appropriation.

In 1927, Hirshberg became director of the Akron Public Library but remained only until 1929, when he was appointed to the combined position of dean of the School of Library Science and director of libraries at Western Reserve University. One of his first steps was to merge the two largest libraries, those of Case and of Adelbert College. He collaborated with Robert Binkley in the creation of a regional union catalog to record the holdings of Western Reserve, Oberlin, Ohio State, the University of Michigan, the University of Cincinnati, and other libraries.

Hirshberg retired as dean in 1943 and as director of libraries at Western Reserve in 1945. Throughout his career, he was active in professional organizations, holding offices and serving on committees.

HODGES, NATHANIEL DANA CARLILE (1852-1927) was a native of Salem, Massachusetts. He graduated from Harvard in 1874 and spent a year and a half as a student at the University of Heidelberg. In 1895, he became an assistant at the Astor Library in New York. Two years later, he moved on to the Harvard Library, where he was assigned to classifying scientific books. In 1900, he was appointed librarian of the Cincinnati Public Library, where he remained until his retirement in 1924. The library's services were expanded extensively to reach all of the people during his administration through the creation of twenty-six branches, fifty-six deposit stations, and 116 school stations.

Hodges was president of the Ohio Library Association from 1904 to 1905 and was a major figure in the affairs of the American Library Association, serving as ALA president in 1909-1910.

HOLLEY, EDWARD GAILON (1927-   ) was born in Pulaski, Tennessee. He graduated from David Lipscomb College in 1949 and completed a master's degree at George Peabody College in library science and English in 1951. He had worked as a student assistant in the David Lipscomb Library and decided to make a career in librarianship. He entered the University of Illinois to begin work on his doctorate but dropped out for three years for active duty with the U.S Naval Reserves.

Earlier, Holley had been employed in the photographic reproduction laboratory at the University of Illinois. After his return, he was a graduate assistant in the Graduate School of Library Science from 1956 to 1957 and librarian of the education, philosophy, and psychology library for five years, beginning in 1957. He received a Ph.D. in library science in 1961. His dissertation, "Charles Evans, American Bibliographer," was published in 1963 by the University of Illinois Press and won the Scarecrow Press Award of the American Library Association for its "outstanding contribution to library literature."

In 1962, Holley was appointed director of libraries of the University of Houston. During his tenure, the library experienced a phenomenal growth in its book collection, budget, and building space.

Holley resigned his post at the University of Houston in 1971 to become dean of the School of Library Science at the University of North Carolina.

Holley was president of the Texas Library Association in 1971 and was inaugurated as president of the American Library Association at the annual conference in 1974 in New York.

In 1985, Holley retired from the deanship at the University of North Carolina while remaining a member of the library school faculty. In 1987, he was presented with the ALA Lippincott Award and in 1988 the Association of College and Research Libraries Research Academic Librarian of the Year Award.

HOPPER, FRANKLIN FERGUSON (1878-1950) was born in Eatontown, New Jersey. He graduated from Princeton in 1900 and from the Pratt Institute Library School in 1901. His first library position was as a cataloger at the Library of Congress from 1901 to 1903. From 1903 to 1904, he was a branch librarian at the Carnegie Library in Pittsburgh, and from 1904 to 1908, he served as order librarian at the same institution. From 1908 to 1914, he headed the Tacoma (Washington) Public Library. In 1914, Hopper was called to the New York Public Library by Edwin H. Anderson as chief of the order division. One of his first activities was to organize the NYPL Staff Association, of which he was the first president, in 1917. In 1919, Hopper became chief of the New York Public Library's circulation department, a position that enabled him to coordinate and unify a large number of branch libraries scattered throughout the city. Under Hopper's guidance, the library became famous for its work for the foreign-born and for blacks. The library developed notable collections of books from foreign countries.

Hopper became the fourth director of the New York Public Library in 1941 and remained in that position until his retirement in 1946. Among the innovations that occurred at the New York Public Library during Hopper's administration were establishment of readers' advisory and adult education services, beginning of a picture collection and music library, and emphasis on library service for children and young people.

Hopper was active in library associations. He was one of the founders of the Pacific Northwest Library Association and was its president in 1913-1914. He was president of the New York Library Club (1923-1924), president of the New York Library Association (1925-1926), and vice-president of the American Library Association (1935-1936).

One commentator noted that "Franklin Hopper was a national influence in the book world for over forty years."

HORN, ANDREW HARLIS (1914-1983) was born in Ogden, Utah. He graduated from the University of Los Angeles in 1943 and went on to earn M.A. and Ph.D. degrees. He received a B.L.S. from the Berkeley Library School in 1948. After service with the U.S. Army medical department during World War II (1943-1946) and teaching history at UCLA and Johns Hopkins, Horn joined the UCLA library staff as senior library assistant in 1947. He subsequently worked in the special collections department (1948-1950), as university archivist (1950-1954), as assistant librarian (1951-1952), and as associate university librarian (1952-1954). From 1954 to 1957, he was librarian of the University of North Carolina at Chapel Hill. He returned to California as librarian of Occidental College (1957-1959) and held various positions with the UCLA School of Library Service (1959-1983). He served as dean from 1959 to 1966. He participated in a number of major library surveys and was active in various organizations.

HOSMER, JAMES KENDALL (1834-1927), president of the American Library Association from 1902 to 1903, was born in Northfield, Connecticut, and was in military service during the Civil War. He was librarian of the Minneapolis Public Library from 1892 to 1904. The remainder of his long life was spent in writing and scholarship. His extensive writings included novels, biographies, histories, and stories.

HOSTETTER, ANITA MILLER (1889-1963) was born in Ladoga, Indiana. She graduated from the University of Kansas in 1917 and from the University of Illinois Library School in 1920. Her career was devoted to developing and monitoring library education programs throughout the United States from 1925 to 1955. She worked chiefly with the ALA board of education for librarianship during a transition period when standards were being established and schools were undergoing accreditation.

HOWE, HARRIET EMMA (1881-1965) was born in Urbana, Illinois. She graduated from the University of Illinois Library School in 1902 and from Harvard in 1928. She held a variety of positions, chiefly in the field of library education: she was an instructor at the University of Illinois, director of the University of Washington School of Librarianship (1905-1906), head cataloger at the University of Iowa (1906-1910), director of Iowa's summer school for library training (1914-1917), chief cataloger of the Minneapolis Public Library (1910-1913), assistant professor at Western Reserve University (1913-1917), and assistant professor at the Simmons College Library School (1917-1924). She also taught in summer sessions at the Columbia Library School (1920-1923). Miss Howe was further involved in library education from 1924 to 1927 when she served as executive assistant of the ALA board of education for librarianship. She held an associate professorship at the University of Chicago Graduate Library School. To cap her career, she was named in 1931 director of the newly established School of Librarianship at the University of Denver, remaining in that position until her retirement in 1950.

Retirement at Denver, however, did not end Miss Howe's professional career. For two years, starting in 1953, she was acting director of the University of Southern California Library School, and she accepted an appointment to teach cataloging at Florida State University.

Miss Howe was active in professional organizations. She was elected to numerous offices and served on several key committees.

HUNT, CLARA WHITEHILL (1871-1958) was born in New York and graduated from the New York State Library School in 1898. Her primary interest was library services to children. She held positions in Philadelphia and Newark before becoming superintendent of work with children at the Brooklyn Public Library from 1903 until 1939. She was chairman of the ALA children's literature section and author of standard manuals such as *Library Work with Children* (1929) and *What Shall We Read to the Children* (1915).

ISOM, MARY FRANCES (1865-1920) was born in Cleveland, Ohio. She attended Wellesley College and the Pratt Institute Library School. Her first position was with the Portland Library Association, which shortly became the Portland Public Library. She organized the Oregon Library Association in 1904 and was also the prime mover in founding the Pacific Northwest Library Association, which she served as president in 1910-1911. In 1912-1913, she was vice-president of the American Library Association. In 1918-1919, she spent six months in France organizing libraries in American hospitals.

JACKSON, WILLIAM VERNON (1926-   ) was born in Chicago and graduated from Northwestern University. He holds M.A. and Ph.D. degrees in romance languages from Harvard and an M.S. in library science from the University of Illinois. After several years of teaching, he entered the library profession as undergraduate librarian and library school faculty member at the University of Illinois (1952-1962). From 1963 to 1965, he was associate professor of Spanish and Portuguese at the University of Wisconsin. From 1966 to 1970, he was on the faculty of the University of Pittsburgh Library School, and from 1970 to 1978, he was a faculty member at Vanderbilt University.

The U.S. State Department frequently appointed Jackson as a consultant on Latin American affairs, sending him on missions to Argentina, Bolivia, Brazil, Ecuador, Venezuela, Central America, and elsewhere. Similar appointments have come from the Organization for American States, the Peace Corps, and the Library of Congress. An appointment as a Fulbright research scholar took him to France in 1956-1957. One of his primary interests is the study of American library resources, on which he has written extensively. A work on the major libraries of the world is in progress. From 1976 until his retirement in 1988, he was on the faculty of the University of Texas Graduate School of Library and Information Science.

JACOBS, JOHN HALL (1905-1967) was born in Bolivar, Tennessee. He graduated from Memphis State College and received a degree in library science from Emory University in 1933. He was a library assistant at Memphis State while a student and in 1934 became supervisor of the Shelby County (Tennessee) libraries until 1938. In 1938, he was appointed director of the New Orleans

Public Library, where he remained until 1960 except for a period of military service during World War II. He moved to Atlanta, Georgia, in 1960 to become director of the Atlanta and Fulton County Public Library System. He also taught for periods in the library schools at Florida State, Emory, the University of Illinois, and the University of Syracuse.

Jacobs was a leader in several professional organizations: he was president of the Tennessee Library Association, president of the Louisiana Library Association (1947-1948) , president of the Southwestern Library Association (1946-1948), president of the Southeastern Library Association (1967), and chairman of various ALA committees. He served as editor of the *Louisiana Library Association Bulletin* and as associate editor of the *Southeastern Librarian*.

JEFFERSON, THOMAS (1743-1826), often referred to as the father of the Library of Congress, offered to sell his personal library, and in 1815, his library of 6,487 volumes became the property of the U.S. government at a purchase price of $23,950. This transaction more than doubled the size of the library. Outraged critics objected to the cost of the purchase and to the nature of the selection, which, they charged, included too many works in foreign languages, too many that had a philosophical character, some that were "objectionable," and even "books of an atheistical, irreligious, and immoral tendency."

Jefferson was also responsible for developing the first classification scheme adopted by the Library of Congress. It divided all knowledge into forty-four subject divisions and was followed by the library for the next hundred years.

On June 1, 1989, the *New York Times* reported that the long-lost catalog of Jefferson's library, in manuscript, had been discovered by two scholars and was printed for the first time by the Library of Congress.

JENNINGS, JUDSON (1872-1948), a native of Schenectady, New York, attended the New York State Library School in Albany in 1897. He was with the New York State Library from 1899 to 1903 and again from 1906 to 1907. From 1903 to 1906, he was librarian of the Duquesne (Pennsylvania) Public Library. He spent the remaining thirty-five years of his active librarianship, 1907 to 1942, as librarian of the Seattle Public Library, which he pioneered into a large metropolitan library.

Jennings was the first president of the Washington Library Association in 1932. He was one of the founders of the Pacific Northwest Library Association and was its president in 1909-1910. He was elected ALA president in 1923-1924. In 1919, he went to Germany to establish a library for the American army of occupation. His numerous journal articles and books mainly concerned adult education and library service for children.

JESSE, WILLIAM HERMAN (1908-1970) was born in Versailles, Kentucky, and graduated from the University of Kentucky in 1923. He was employed by the Johnson County, Kentucky, public schools in a combination job that included being school librarian. He earned a B.S. in library science from Columbia in 1938 and went to Brown University until 1942 as chief of the readers' division. He spent a short time as assistant library director at the University of Nebraska before transferring to a department headship in the U.S. Department of Agriculture Library in Washington, D.C. Almost immediately, Jesse was offered and accepted the directorship of the University of Tennessee Library, where he was destined to remain for the next quarter century. During this period, Jesse developed one of the most active careers as a consultant on library buildings. He also inaugurated an annual lecture series, bringing prominent librarians to the Tennessee campus to present talks on subjects of current interest that were subsequently published. His active participation in library organizations included a term as president of the Southeastern Library Association from 1946 to 1948.

JEWETT, CHARLES COFFIN (1816-1868) was a native of Maine who graduated from Brown University in 1835. He was secretary and librarian of the recently founded Smithsonian Institution. In 1850, the Smithsonian published his *Notices of Public Libraries in the United States of America*, the first comprehensive collection of facts and statistics on American libraries. Jewett proposed a nationwide union catalog of American libraries and centralized cataloging, but both ideas were ahead of their time and did not mature until later. Jewett spent the last ten years of his life as superintendent of the Boston Public Library, for which he selected and purchased books.

JOECKEL, CARLETON BRUNS (1886-1960) was born in Lake Mills, Wisconsin, and became one of the great teachers of library science. He graduated from the University of Wisconsin in 1908 and from the New York State Library School at Albany in 1910. His first professional job was secretary for a year to the librarian of the St. Louis Public Library, followed by three years as assistant reference librarian and superintendent of circulation at the University of California Library at Berkeley. In 1914, he was appointed librarian of the Berkeley Public Library, where he remained until 1927 except for two years, 1917-1919, when he served in the U.S. Army during World War I.

Joeckel's entry into teaching came when he taught part-time in the School of Librarianship at the University of California. He joined the faculty at the University of Michigan Library School in 1927. He completed a Ph.D. at the University of Chicago Graduate Library School in 1934 and left Michigan in 1935 to accept an appointment as professor of library science at the University of Chicago. He showed exceptional talent over the next ten years in teaching and in directing student research.

Joeckel found time also for extensive research and writing on his own, providing such landmark works as the *Government of the American Public Library* (1935), *A National Plan for Public*

Library Service (in collaboration with Amy Winslow) (1948), and *A Metropolitan Library in Action* (based on a survey of the Chicago Public Library) (1940).

Joeckel was active in several professional organizations, serving as president of the California Library Association from 1919 to 1920, as president of the Michigan Library Association from 1930 to 1931, and as second vice-president of the American Library Association from 1936 to 1937.

When Louis Round Wilson retired in 1942, Joeckel was named dean of the University of Chicago Graduate Library School. He was ably assisted by Leon Carnovsky as assistant dean and by Pierce Butler and Lowell A. Martin. In 1945, at age sixty, Joeckel retired and returned to Berkeley as a member of the School of Librarianship. Declining health forced him to retire in 1950.

A biographer, Thomas S. Harding, comments that "Joeckel is a significant figure in American Librarianship not only for his own contributions, but also for the impact he made on his colleagues and students."

JONES, CLARA STANTON (1913-) was born in St. Louis, Missouri. She graduated from Spelman College in Atlanta in 1934 and from the University of Michigan School of Library Science in 1938. She began as a student assistant and later as an assistant in the catalog and reference departments of the Atlanta University Library. Two years later, she moved to Dillard University to become a reference library assistant. In 1940, Mrs. Jones was appointed associate librarian of the Southern University Library in Baton Rouge, Louisiana. She made a key move in 1944 by joining the staff of the Detroit Public Library as a children's librarian, a young adult librarian, and an adult librarian specializing in readers' services. Other promotions followed: she was appointed chief of the readers' services department in 1963, library neighborhood consultant (a new post) in 1968, and finally, in 1970, director of the Detroit Public Library system — the first woman and the first black to hold that position.

Mrs. Jones was prematurely elevated to the presidency of the American Library Association in April 1976 following the death of the incumbent president, Allie Beth Martin. She was inaugurated officially during the ALA centennial conference in Chicago in July 1976.

Recognition for Mrs. Jones's achievements have come from various sources: she received the Award for Distinguished Service to Librarianship from the ALA Black Caucus in 1970, the Golden State Achievement Award for service to the community from the Golden State Mutual Life Insurance Company, and the Distinguished Alumnus Award of the University of Michigan School of Library Science.

JONES, VIRGINIA LACY (1912-1984) was born in Cincinnati, Ohio. She graduated from Hampton Institute in 1936 and from the University of Illinois Library School in 1938. She received a Ph.D. degree from the University of Chicago in 1945. She was librarian of the Louisville Municipal College from 1933 to 1939 and cataloging librarian at Atlanta University from 1939 to 1941. From 1941 to 1943, she was an instructor at the Atlanta University School of Library Service. In 1945, she was promoted to the deanship with the rank of professor, gaining ALA accreditation for the school. She remained as dean until 1981. During her tenure, the Atlanta school graduated about 1,800 black librarians. After her retirement in 1981, she was appointed the first director of the Robert W. Woodruff Library at the Atlanta University Center. Miss Jones was the first black to be elected president of the Association of American Library Schools. From the American Library Association, she received the Melvil Dewey Medal, the Lippincott Award, and honorary membership.

KAISER, JOHN BOYNTON (1887-1973) was born in Cleveland, Ohio. He graduated from Western Reserve University in 1908 and held two degrees (1910 and 1917) from the New York State Library School. While in Albany, he was employed at the New York State Law Library, and in 1910-1911 he was assistant librarian of the Texas State Library in Austin. From 1911 to 1914, he was a departmental librarian at the University of Illinois, after which he became librarian of the Tacoma (Washington) Public Library for ten years. He made a switch to academic librarianship when he was appointed director of libraries and of the library school at Iowa State University. He remained there until 1927. He was then chosen as librarian of the Oakland (California) Public Free Library. His next move was in 1942, when Kaiser was selected to be director of the Newark (New Jersey) Public Library until 1958. In each position he made far-reaching improvements in organization and management.

Kaiser wrote extensively on subjects such as civil service, personnel staff practices, and legal aspects of library service. Kaiser's participation in professional organizations included a term as president of the New Jersey Library Association, (1948-1949) and as vice-president of the American Library Association (1949-1950). While at Tacoma, he served as president of the Pacific Northwest Library Association (1917-1918).

KASER, DAVID (1924-   ) was born in Mishawaka, Indiana, graduated from Houghton College in 1949, and received an M.A. degree from the University of Notre Dame in 1950. In 1952, he completed a master's degree in library science from the University of Michigan and in 1956 was awarded a Ph.D. degree. He was on the staff of the Ball State University Library (1952-1954); on the University of Michigan library staff (1954-1956); and chief of acquisitions (1956-1959) and assistant director (1959-1960) of the Washington University libraries in St. Louis. From 1960 to 1968, he was director of libraries at Vanderbilt University, and from 1968 to 1973, he was director of libraries at Cornell University. From 1973 to 1989, Kaser was on the faculty of the Indiana University Library School at Bloomington. He has held a number of foreign assignments in Ireland, Korea, Laos, Indonesia, Nigeria, France, and Saudi Arabia.

Kaser was editor of the *Missouri Library Association Quarterly* from 1958 to 1960 and of *College and Research Libraries* from 1963 to 1969. In 1968-1969, he was president of the Association of College and Research Libraries.

KEOGH, ANDREW (1869-1953) was born in Newcastle-upon-Tyne, England, and educated at Durham College of Science. As a youth, he joined the staff of the Newcastle-upon-Tyne Public Library. Seeking further professional advancement, he emigrated to the United States in 1899. His first job was as a librarian of the Linonian and Brothers Library at Yale. A year later, he was appointed reference librarian. In 1904, he received an M.A. degree at Yale, and in 1912, he was made assistant librarian. After the sudden death of John Schwab, Keogh was named librarian of Yale in 1916.

The planning of the Sterling Memorial Library, the principal Yale library, was Keogh's chief concern until its dedication in 1931. His effective relations with alumni and leading book collectors led to outstanding gifts and acquisitions by the Yale Library.

Keogh was elected president of the American Library Association for the 1929-1930 term.

KNOLLENBERG, BERNHARD (1892-1973) was born in Richmond, Indiana, and held degrees from Earlham College and Harvard University. He was admitted to the bar in 1916 and practiced law until 1938. From 1938 to 1944, he served as librarian of Yale University. Afterward, he filled several governmental posts: he was a consulting expert for the U.S. Treasury, deputy administrator of the Lend Lease Administration of the Office of Strategic Services, and U.S. commissioner for Northwest Atlantic Fisheries. He was the author of several works concerning the American Revolution.

Koch, Theodore Wesley (1871-1941), born in Philadelphia, graduated from the University of Pennsylvania in 1892 and was widely admired as a librarian, translator, bibliographer, and civic leader. At Harvard in 1893 and 1894, he earned two additional degrees, an A.B. and an A.M. in romance languages. He spent five years at Cornell University compiling the monumental *Catalogue of the Dante Collection Presented by Willard Fiske*, published in two volumes in 1898-1900. For two years, 1900 to 1901, Koch was a student at the University of Paris. After his return in 1902, he became an assistant at the Library of Congress catalog division. In 1904, Koch began a connection with the University of Michigan that continued until 1915. He spent a year (1904) as assistant librarian and was university librarian from 1905 to 1915. An administrative dispute caused Koch to resign, and in 1916, he returned to the Library of Congress as chief of the order division. In 1919, he was appointed librarian of Northwestern University, where he achieved an outstanding reputation until his death in 1941. One of his principal accomplishments was the planning and erection of the Charles Deering Library building in 1929.

Koch was involved with a number of library organizations: he was president of the Michigan Library Association, president of the Chicago Library Club (1927), secretary-treasurer of the American Library Association (1922-1924), and ALA president (1931-1933). He was a delegate to the British Library Association's fiftieth anniversary meeting in 1927.

Koopman, Harry Lyman (1860-1937) was born in Freeport, Maine, graduated from Colby College in 1880, and received an M.A. degree from Harvard in 1893. He served as a clerk in the Astor Library in New York (1881-1882), and as a cataloger at Cornell University (1883-1884), at Columbia College (1884-1885), at Rutgers (1885-1886), and at the University of Vermont (1886-1892). In 1893, he was appointed librarian of Brown University, a post that he filled for thirty-seven years. A gift from Andrew Carnegie financed construction of the new John Hay Library, opened in 1910 and planned by Koopman.

Koopman was president of the American Library Institute from 1928 to 1930, president of the Massachusetts Library Club from 1900 to 1901, and president of the Rhode Island Library Association from 1904 to 1907. His writings include numerous contributions on bibliography, printing, and literary subjects.

Kroger, Alice Bertha (1864-1909) was born in St. Louis, Missouri. She joined the staff of the St. Louis Public Library in 1882 and attended the New York State Library School in 1889. She was appointed librarian of Drexel Institute in Philadelphia in 1891, and the following year, she opened a library school, the third in the country, with herself as director.

Miss Kroger is best known for her *Guide to the Study and Use of Reference Books*, which has been revised frequently, most recently by Isadore Mudge, Constance Winchell, and Eugene P. Sheehy.

Kuhlman, Augustus Frederick (1889-1986) was a native of Hubbard, Iowa. He graduated from Northwestern College in 1916 and held master's and doctoral degrees in sociology from the University of Chicago. After several years in a teaching career, he became associate director of libraries at the University of Chicago from 1929 to 1936. He spent the remainder of his career as director of the Joint University Libraries at Nashville, Tennessee, from 1936 to 1960.

Kuhlman was president of the Tennessee Library Association from 1954 to 1955. He was widely known as a surveyor of individual libraries and for regional studies. He was author of a standard work, *Guide to Material on Crime and Criminal Justice* (1929). A 1935 survey by Kuhlman resulted in the establishment of the Joint University Libraries to serve Vanderbilt University and George Peabody College. He was ninety-seven at the time of his death.

LANCOUR, HAROLD (1908-1981) was born in Duluth, Minnesota, and graduated from the University of Washington in 1935. He received B.S. and M.S. degrees in library science from Columbia University (1946-1948). He began his professional career as a reference assistant at the New York Public Library from 1935 to 1937 and as librarian of Cooper Union from 1937 to 1947. From 1947 to 1961, Lancour was associate director of the University of Illinois Library School. From 1961 until his retirement in 1974, he was dean of the newly established library school at the University of Pittsburgh.

Lancour had extensive international experience, carrying out library surveys in Nigeria, Sierra Leone, Gambia, Liberia, Mali, Guatemala, Iran, and Chile. He served for several years as director of the International Graduate Summer School at the College of Librarianship in Wales. His other professional activities included being chairman of the ALA board of education for librarianship (1954-1957), managing editor of *Library Trends* (1952-1962), the first editor of the *Journal of Education for Librarianship* (1960-1963), coeditor of the *Encyclopedia of Library and Information Science* (1969), and a founder of Beta Phi Mu, the international honor society for librarians.

One of Lancour's major achievements was to promote close Anglo-American relations in library education, starting with his spending a year, 1950-1951, as a Fulbright scholar in Britain. He promoted an active exchange of English librarians, including J. Clement Harrison, Roy Stokes, and Frank Hogg, to visit and teach in U.S. schools. Norman Horrocks came from western Australia in 1963. Lancour also had a decisive effect upon library education in West Africa.

LANE, WILLIAM COOLIDGE (1859-1937), a native of Massachusetts and a graduate of Harvard, succeeded Justin Winsor as librarian of Harvard. He had worked in the Harvard library from 1881 to 1887 and became assistant librarian in charge of the catalog from 1887 to 1893. He was librarian of the Boston Athenaeum from 1893 to 1898 and then returned to Harvard as librarian until his retirement in 1928.

Lane was president of the American Library Association in 1898-1899. He promoted the appointment of Herbert Putnam as librarian of Congress. He was a voluminous writer, coeditor of the ALA portrait index, and author of numerous other works.

LARNED, JOSEPHUS NELSON (1836-1913) began his library career as superintendent of the Buffalo (New York) Young Men's Association Library from 1877 to 1897. In this position, he started one of the first children's rooms and opened the library on Sunday. He was a prolific writer, completing the monumental *History for Ready Reference* (1901-1910) in seven volumes. Larned was president of the American Library Association in 1893-1894.

LEGLER, HENRY EDWARD (1861-1917) was born in Palermo, Sicily, and emigrated with his family to the United States shortly after the Civil War. His early career was spent in journalism as a reporter for and editor of the *Milwaukee Sentinel*. His connection with libraries began in 1904, when he was appointed secretary of the Wisconsin Free Library Commission. He became secretary of the University of Wisconsin extension division. The Legislative Reference Bureau, which he opened in the capital, became a model of its kind.

In 1905, Legler was elected chairman of the League of Library Commissions. For the American Library Association he was an active chairman of the publishing board, a connection that culminated in his election as ALA president in 1912-1913.

In 1909, Legler became librarian of the Chicago Public Library. During that period, an agreement was reached for two large reference centers to specialize: Newberry was to concentrate on history and the arts, and John Crerar on the sciences and technology. The Chicago Public Library experienced phenomenal growth during Legler's administration: home use of books grew from 1.8 million to 6 million, branches grew from one to forty, a music department was opened, and Legler cooperated in setting up 200 classroom libraries and branches in several high schools. A regional plan for branch libraries resulted in the establishment of five regional branches in each large division of the metropolitan area.

LEIBNIZ, GOTTFIED WILHELM (1646-1716) studied at Leipzig and Jena universities. In 1676, he became librarian of the Duke of Brunswick's collections in Hannover and Wolfenbuttel. He continued in that position for forty years. The libraries under his direction increased substantially in size. His ideal was a complete, well-ordered library, and he regularly acquired new books and periodicals, utilizing practical cataloging and classification schemes.

Leibniz was a leading scientist of his time. He developed the infinitesimal calculus, published ten years before Sir Isaac Newton's version.

LOCKE, GEORGE HERBERT (1870-1937), a leading Canadian librarian for many years, was born in Beamsville, Ontario, and graduated from the University of Toronto in 1893. After a teaching career, which included serving as dean of the School of Education at the University of Chicago and at McGill University between 1899 and 1908, Locke was appointed director of the Toronto Public Library, a position that he filled for nearly thirty years. During his administration, the staff grew from 26 to 232, a new central building was erected, and branches were expanded from four to sixteen.

Locke was elected to the presidency of the American Library Association for the 1926-1927 term. In 1927, he was the principal speaker at the Jubilee Conference of the British Library Association in Edinburgh. He was instrumental in developing service to children in the Toronto system. Throughout his career, he emphasized the library as an educational institution.

LOGASA, HANNAH (1879-1967) was born in Rock Island, Illinois. She graduated from the University of Chicago quite late, in 1921. She began her library career as a general assistant at the Omaha Public Library in 1904, from which she went on in 1914 to become a high school librarian at the University of Chicago. For the next twenty-five years, she worked to develop one of the pioneer laboratory school libraries. She produced several publications, such as *Biography in Collections, Historical Fiction*, and *Science for Youth*. She was also a guest instructor at many schools.

LOHRER, ALICE (1907-   ) is a native of Chicago and a 1928 graduate of the University of Chicago. She also holds degrees in library science from the University of Illinois and the University of Chicago. She began her library career as a school librarian in Oak Park and Hinsdale high schools and was a visiting instructor for summer sessions at Purdue University, the University of Southern California, the University of West Virginia, the University of Wisconsin, and the University of Denver at various times between 1939 and 1966. Miss Lohrer was appointed to the University of Illinois Library School faculty and remained in that position until her retirement. She has filled a number of foreign assignments: as a Fulbright lecturer in Bangkok, Thailand, from 1955 to 1956;

at the Japan Library School of Keio University in Tokyo in 1959; and as a Fulbright lecturer at the University of Tehran, Iran from 1966 to 1967.

Miss Lohrer was president of the Illinois Association of High School Librarians and president of the Illinois Library Association. She had a total of fifty-nine years of professional activity.

Miss Lohrer was the 1987 recipient of the American Association of School Librarians' President's Award. The citation reads: "An annual award of $3,000 presented to an individual who has demonstrated excellence and provided an outstanding national or international contribution to school librarianship and school library media development. Donated by Baker and Taylor. Administered by the American Association of School Librarians."

LORD, MILTON EDWARD (1898-1985) was born in Lynn, Massachusetts, and graduated from Harvard in 1919. He was a student from 1925 to 1926 at the Ecole des Sciences Politiques in Paris. He began his professional career as an assistant at the Harvard College Library (1919-1925), as librarian of the Harvard Union (1919-1923), and as librarian at the American Academy in Rome (1926-1930). He was the director of university libraries and of the library school at the State University of Iowa from 1930 to 1932. Lord became director of the Boston Public Library in 1932 and remained in that position until his retirement in 1965. He was the librarian-in-residence (1971-1974) and director of libraries at the State University of Iowa (1975-1976). He was in military service from 1918 to 1924.

Lord received many honors. He was president of the Massachusetts Library Association from 1965 to 1966 and president of the American Library Association from 1949 to 1950.

LORENZ, JOHN GEORGE (1915-), a native of New York City, graduated from the City College of New York in 1939 and from the Columbia School of Library Service in 1940. As an undergraduate, Lorenz had worked as an assistant in the education department of the Brooklyn Public Library. From 1940 to 1944, he was on the staffs of the Queens Borough and Schenectady public libraries. In 1944, he was appointed chief of the reference division of the Grand Rapids Public Library. Two years later, he became assistant state librarian of the Michigan State Library in Lansing, with wide-ranging duties. Another opening came in 1957, when Lorenz was appointed assistant director of the library services branch of the U.S. Office of Education, concerned with the new federal library grant program. The next year, 1958, he became director, and he continued in this position until 1963. In 1964, he was named director of the division of library services and educational facilities.

A key move for Lorenz came in 1965, when he was appointed deputy librarian of Congress, second in command at the Library of Congress, until 1976. He was executive director of the Association of Research Libraries from 1976 to 1980, interim director of libraries at the Catholic University of America from 1982 to 1983, special assistant to the librarian of Georgetown University from 1985 to 1987, and interim director of the Washington Research Library Consortium from 1987 to the present.

LOW, EDMON (1902-1983) was born in Kiowa, Oklahoma. He graduated from East Central State College in 1926 and held library science degrees from the University of Illinois (1930) and the University of Michigan (1938). From 1926 to 1937, he was assistant librarian of East Central State College in Ada, Oklahoma, and from 1938 to 1940, he was librarian of Bowling Green (Ohio) State University. In 1940, he became director of the Oklahoma State University Library at Stillwater and held that position until 1967. He taught in summer sessions at the University of Michigan intermittently from 1967 to 1972. After retirement from Oklahoma State University, Low was librarian of New College in Sarasota, Florida, from 1972 to 1975, and of the University of South Florida's Sarasota campus from 1975 to 1980. He was president of the Southwestern Library Association (1950-1952), president of the Association of College and Research Libraries (1960-1961), president of the Oklahoma Library Association (1949), and vice-president of the American Library Association (1962-1963).

Low was highly successful as a lobbyist for library legislation before congressional committees, gaining the title of ALA legislative "warrior."

As a fitting memorial, Oklahoma State University named its library the Edmon Low Library.

LOWRIE, JEAN ELIZABETH (1918-) was born in Northville, New York, and graduated in 1940 from Keuka College in Keuka Park, New York. She received a degree in library science from Western Reserve University in 1941. She began her library experience as a children's librarian in the Toledo (Ohio) Public Library from 1941 to 1944. From 1944 to 1951, she was an elementary school librarian in Oak Ridge, Tennessee, during which time, from 1948 to 1949, she was an exchange teacher-librarian in Nottingham, England. In 1951, she became librarian at the campus elementary school of Western Michigan University and remained there until 1956. She joined the faculty of Western Michigan in the department of librarianship in 1958 and assumed the directorship of the School of Librarianship in 1963 until 1983. She received a Ph.D. degree in 1959.

Miss Lowrie has held various offices in library organizations: she was president of the American Association of School Librarians (1963-1964), president of the International Association of School Librarians (1971-1974), and president of the American Library Association (1973-1974).

LUDINGTON, FLORA BELLE (1898-1967) was born in Michigan and attended Whitman College in Walla Walla, Washington. She earned a B.A. degree in librarianship from the University of Washington in 1920, a master's degree in history from Mills College in Oakland, California, and a B.L.S. degree from the New

York State Library School in 1925. She began her library career as an assistant in the circulation department, from 1920 to 1921, at the University of Washington, followed by a position as reference librarian at Mills College. She then became an associate professor of bibliography and an associate librarian at Mills.

In 1936, she accepted an appointment as librarian of Mount Holyoke College in South Hadley, Massachusetts. She also taught for summer schools at Columbia and elsewhere. She was instrumental in establishing the Hampshire Inter-Library Center, a cooperative plan to serve Amherst, Smith, and Mount Holyoke colleges.

During a leave of absence from her Mount Holyoke position from 1944 to 1946, Miss Ludington was the first director of the U.S. Information Library in Bombay, India. In 1948, she served as a visiting expert on information libraries for the Supreme Command for the Allied Powers (SCAP) in Japan. She also traveled extensively in Africa under State Department auspices.

Miss Ludington was long active in the American Library Association and served as ALA president in 1953-1954. At the ALA's annual conference in Los Angeles, over which she presided, the association joined with the American Book Publishers Council in endorsing the celebrated declaration "Freedom to Read" and a resolution on freedom from censorship of U.S. overseas libraries. A certificate of achievement was conferred on her in 1948 by SCAP in Japan.

LYDENBERG, HARRY MILLER (1874-1960) was born in Dayton, Ohio. He attended Harvard on a scholarship and worked in the university library. Earlier, he had been a page in the Dayton Public Library. He graduated from Harvard in three years in 1897. His lifetime association with the New York Public Library began in 1896, when he was employed as a cataloger at the Lenox Library (which later merged with the NYPL). John Shaw Billings, the director, recognized Lydenberg's potentialities and made him responsible for classifying and arranging books. He put him in charge of the manuscript collection and in 1899 promoted him to the position of assistant to the director. Other steps in Lydenberg's advancement were appointment as reference librarian (chief of the research collections) in 1908, as assistant director in 1928, and as director in 1934 after Edwin H. Anderson's retirement. Lydenberg organized the move in 1911 to the monumental new central building on Forty-Second Street and Fifth Avenue.

Lyndenberg put strong emphasis on developing the library's collections, resulting in holdings that reached nearly three million volumes by the time he retired in 1941 — three times the total in 1907. To ensure adequate coverage, Lydenberg himself spent five months in Western Europe, Eastern Europe, and the Soviet Union in 1923-1924 collecting books.

Lydenberg was a leader in several landmark bibliographical projects, such as the first edition of the *Union List of Serials in the United States and Canada* (1924-1926), the first *Census of Fifteenth Century Books Owned in America* (1918-1919), and completion of Joseph Sabin's *Bibliotheca Americana.*

Lydenberg was elected president of the American Library Association for 1932-1933 and president of the Bibliographical Society of America from 1929 to 1931. He was one of the founders of the Association of Research Libraries. He received the ALA Lippincott Award in 1949 in recognition of notable achievements in librarianship.

Lydenberg's final professional positions were to serve as director-librarian of the new Bibliotica Benjamin Franklin in Mexico City from 1941 to 1943 and to direct the new International Relations Office of the American Library Association from 1943 to 1946.

Lydenberg was author of the definitive biography of John Shaw Billings (1924) and *History of the New York Public Library* (1923).

LYLE, GUY REDVERS (1907-   ) was born in the Canadian province of Saskatchewan. After graduating from the University of Alberta, during which he worked at the Edmonton Public

Library, he enrolled in Columbia's School of Library Service and was employed at the New York Public Library as a stack supervisor. His first academic appointment was as library director at Antioch College in Yellow Springs, Ohio. He then assumed the librarianship of the University of North Carolina Women's College at Greensboro and taught in several universities. In 1944, Lyle became library director at Louisiana State University and ten years later moved on to become director of the Emory University Library in Atlanta. His professional activities were varied: he was president of the North Carolina Library Association and chairman of the ACRL board of directors, and he promoted a union catalog of the Atlanta-Athens area.

Lyle is widely known in the academic world for authoring *The Administration of the College Library*, a standard work in its field that has gone through several editions.

Lyle's autobiography, *Beyond My Expectations,* was published in 1981.

LYNCH, BEVERLY P. (1936-   ), librarian of the University of Illinois in Chicago from 1977 to 1989, became dean of the University of California at Los Angeles School of Library and Information Science on September 1, 1989. She holds degrees from North Dakota State University and the University of Illinois Library School and a Ph.D. from the University of Wisconsin. She has served as a staff member at the University of Illinois, at Marquette University, at the Plymouth (England) Public Library, and at Yale University. She was executive secretary of the Association of College and Research Libraries from 1972 to 1976 and served as president of the American Library Association in 1985-1986. She was named ACRL's Academic Research Librarian of the Year in 1981 and won the University of Illinois Graduate School of Library and Information's first Distinguished Alumnus Award in 1987. She has taught in the library schools of the University of Wisconsin, the University of Texas, and the University of Chicago. Other contributions include writings on library management and the editing of several books.

MacLeish, Archibald (1892-1982) was appointed librarian of Congress by President Franklin Roosevelt. MacLeish had an established reputation as a poet, playwright, journalist, teacher, lawyer, and government official. His brief tenure as librarian of Congress lasted only five years, from 1939 to 1944. During that time, his major achievement as librarian was to extensively reorganize administrative procedures affecting all operations. MacLeish's nomination was opposed by the library profession because he was not a professional librarian. Nevertheless, the appointment was confirmed by the Senate. Outside experts were brought in to review technical operations. Roosevelt called upon MacLeish for other responsibilities in addition to that of librarian. MacLeish became director of a new war agency, the Office of Facts and Figures, and he drafted speeches and letters for the President. Later, he was assistant secretary of state for public and cultural relations and chairman of the U.S. delegation that established UNESCO. When MacLeish retired in 1944, the position of librarian was offered to Julian Boyd, Princeton University librarian, who declined it. From 1949 to 1967, MacLeish taught at Harvard and at Amherst College.

MacPherson, Harriet Dorothea (1892-1967) was born in College Point, New York, and graduated from Wellesley College in 1914. She attended Columbia University from 1924 to 1929 and received master's and Ph.D. degrees in modern languages. She also attended the University of Nancy and the Sorbonne in France from 1923 to 1925. She received her library education at the New York Public Library and had a library career of fifty years, from 1917 to 1967. From 1917 to 1924, she was a cataloger and reviser at the Columbia University Library, and she was head cataloger at the City College of New York from 1924 to 1928. In

1927-1943, she taught cataloging at Columbia. She left that position to serve as librarian of Smith College at Northampton, Massachusetts, until 1949, when she joined the faculty of the Drexel Institute of Technology Library School in Philadelphia, where she spent the last decade of her active professional career. She served as dean of the school and director of libraries at Drexel until her retirement in 1958.

Miss MacPherson was president of the ALA library education division from 1950 to 1951 and was vice-president of the American Library Association. She was a long-time member of the Dewey decimal classification committee and an active chairman of the ALA cataloging section.

MAGRUDER, PATRICK (1768-1819) was the second librarian of Congress. He took over after Beckley, who had been another Jefferson appointee, died in 1807. His appointment was in the nature of an interim tour of duty. After Jefferson's books were received, Magruder was asked to resign in 1815.

MANN, MARGARET (1878-1960) was born in Cedar Rapids, Iowa. She studied for two years at the Armour Institute department of library economy, directed by Katharine Sharp. She worked for a year as a cataloger at the Armour Library, but when the Armour school was transferred to the University of Illinois in 1897, she accompanied Miss Sharp to the new location. For six years at Illinois, under Katharine Sharp's direction and with colleagues such as Isadore Mudge and Minnie E. Sears, she served as assistant librarian and senior instructor, completely revising the clasification and cataloging of the entire Illinois collection.

In 1902, Margaret Mann accepted an offer to head the catalog department of the Carnegie Library of Pittsburgh. She made another move in 1919 when Harrison Carver persuaded her to come to New York to reorganize and recatalog the collections of the Engineering Societies Library, a task that occupied her for the next five years, until 1924. During that time, she also taught part-time at the New York Public Library School. She spent two years, 1924 to 1926, teaching cataloging and classification at the Paris Library School, sponsored by the American Library Association.

In 1926, following her return to the United States, William Warner Bishop appointed Miss Mann to the faculty of the newly formed library school at the University of Michigan, where she remained until her retirement in 1938. She was active in the American Library Association, serving as its first vice-president in 1924. Her text, *Introduction to Cataloging and Classification of Books*, has been regarded as a standard work since its publication in 1930.

A prize award, administered by the ALA resources and technical services division, is the Margaret Mann Citation, presented annually "to a cataloger or classifier for outstanding professional achievement in the areas of cataloging or classification."

MARSHALL, ALBERT PRINCE (1914-) was born in Texarkana, Texas, and graduated from Lincoln University in 1938. He earned a B.S. in library science from the University of Illinois in 1950 and an M.A. in history from the University of Missouri in 1959. In 1939-1941, he was assistant librarian of Lincoln University, and from 1941 to 1950, he was librarian of the State Teacher's College at Winston-Salem, North Carolina. From 1950 to 1969, he served as librarian of Lincoln University. In 1969, he became director of the Eastern Michigan University Library.

Marshall was president of the Missouri Library Association in 1961-1962.

MARTEL, CHARLES (1860-1945) was born in Zurich, Switzerland. He visited the United States at the time of the Philadelphia Centennial Exposition in 1876. In 1892, he accepted a job at the Newberry Library, working with Poole and Hanson. In 1897, he moved on to the Library of Congress, where he served as chief classifier from 1897 to 1912 and as chief of the cataloging division until his retirement in 1930. From then until his death at age eighty-five in 1945, he was a consultant in cataloging, classification, and bibliography. He spent five months in Rome in 1928 in company with Hanson, Bishop, and Cardinal Tisserant to modernize the Vatican Library's cataloging and classification systems.

MARTIN, ALLIE BETH DENT (1914-1976) was a native of Annieville, Arkansas, and graduated from Arkansas College in 1935. She launched her career as a librarian by being a student assistant at the college library. She was librarian of Batesville's first public library before moving to Little Rock in 1936 to become librarian of Little Rock Junior College. In 1937-1938, she was assistant to the secretary of the Arkansas Library Commission, a new state agency. In 1939, Mrs. Martin earned a degree from the George Peabody School of Library Science. After moving to Tulsa, Oklahoma, in 1949, she joined the staff of the Tulsa Public Library.

From 1953 to 1954, Mrs. Martin edited the *Oklahoma Librarian* and was elected president of the Oklahoma Library Association for the 1955-1956 term. In 1962, she was named director of the Tulsa City-County Library. In 1969-1970, she served as president of the Southwestern Library Association. She died in April 1976 before her term as ALA president was completed.

MARTIN, LOWELL ARTHUR (1912-   ) was born in Chicago and graduated from the Illinois Institute of Technology in 1937. He holds three degrees from the University of Chicago, a B.S., an A.M., and a Ph.D. He began his library career as an assistant in a high school library from 1933 to 1935. He then became assistant librarian of Wright City College from 1935 to 1937, executive assistant to the librarian of the Chicago Public Library from 1941 to 1943, a faculty member at the University of Chicago from 1943 to 1946, and associate dean of the School of Library Service at Columbia University from 1947 to 1953. From 1954 to 1958, he was dean of the Graduate School of Library Service at Rutgers University, and he was vice-president of Grolier, Inc. from 1959 to 1968. He was appointed to the Columbia faculty as a professor in 1969. Martin is a veteran surveyor of large library systems and is the author of several works concerning public library administration.

McANALLY, ARTHUR MONROE (1911-1972) was born in Delaware, Arkansas, and began his higher education at the University of Arkansas. He transferred to the University of Oklahoma, where he completed three degrees, including a B.A. in library science (1933-1936). He continued his library education at the University of Chicago Graduate Library School, from which he received a master's degree (1941) and a Ph.D. (1951). He began his professional career as a student assistant at the University of Oklahoma Library, after which he became supervisor of libraries, from 1935 to 1938, for the junior college and public schools in Edinburg, Texas. He then served as assistant librarian of University College at Northwestern University (1938-1939), as assistant librarian of Knox College (1939-1941), as librarian of Bradley University (1941-1944), as librarian of Wisconsin State Teacher's College in Milwaukee (1944-1945), as librarian of the University of New Mexico (1945-1949), as assistant director for public services at the University of Illinois (1949-1951), and finally, as director of libraries at the University of Oklahoma (1951-1972). He also served as director of the University of Oklahoma Library School from 1951 to 1960.

McAnally had two foreign assignments, first in 1948 as director of libraries of the oldest university in the Americas at Lima, Peru, and second, as visiting professor at the Ankara University School of Librarianship from 1963 to 1964.

As director of the University of Oklahoma Library, McAnally's achievements included constructing a major addition to the central university library building, tripling the size of the book collection, establishing notable special collections on the history of science and business, and obtaining faculty status for the library staff.

McAnally participated in the work of various library organizations: he was president of the New Mexico Library Association in 1947, president of the Southwestern Library Association from 1960 to 1962, and president of the Oklahoma Library Association in 1967.

McAnally was an enthusiastic outdoor sportsman. He died from a heart attack while on a hunting expedition in 1972.

McCarthy, Stephen A. (1908-1990), whose library career spanned a half-century, was born in Eden Valley, Minnesota. The peak of his career was undoubtedly the twenty-one years that he spent rehabilitating the Cornell University libraries. His educational background included graduation from Gonzaga University in Spokane, Washington, a bachelor of library science degree from McGill University in Montreal, and a doctorate from the University of Chicago Graduate Library School. His early library experience included a position as assistant librarian at Saint John's College in Minnesota, as a librarian at Northwestern University, as assistant director and later director of the University of Nebraska Library, and, from 1944 to 1946, as assistant director of the Columbia University library system.

When McCarthy was appointed library director of the Cornell University Library in 1946, he found a chaotic situation, described by him as a "library chamber of horrors." There was a mixture of publicly supported professional schools and endowed colleges. Space was completely lacking, acquisition funds were hopelessly inadequate, staff was short and underpaid, and the collections were classified by an antiquated British Museum scheme. The numerous departmental libraries were decentralized.

Under McCarthy, Cornell built a unified library system, the library budget was increased substantially, and strong emphasis was placed on collection development and on cultivation of a trained professional staff. In 1961, a large new central library building was occupied, and the former building, constructed in 1891, was remodeled as an undergraduate library in 1962. Able assistance in the Cornell library renaissance was provided by several McCarthy associates, especially Giles F. Shepherd, Jr., who was an assistant and sometime associate director, and Felix Reichmann, an acquisition librarian. Notable special collections were added, such as the Icelandic and James Joyce materials.

After completion of the Cornell library's modernization (the planning and construction of new buildings and the creation of a unified library system for budget, personnel, services, collections, and facilities), McCarthy retired in 1967 to become executive director of the Association of Research Libraries, a position in which he remained until December 1974. In the ARL, McCarthy took the lead in establishing and promoting programs and legislation to benefit research libraries in the United States and Canada.

Among his professional activities, McCarthy was president of the Nebraska Library Association in 1940 and president of the New York Library Association in 1951-1952. He spent the year 1953 in Egypt as a Fulbright lecturer and library surveyor. He also participated in a number of college and university library surveys in the United States and Canada.

McCoy, Ralph Edward (1915-   ) was born in St. Louis, Missouri, and graduated from Illinois Wesleyan University in 1937. He holds three degrees from the University of Illinois Library School, including a Ph.D. in 1956. He was a high school librarian in Marissa, Illinois (1937-1938), assistant librarian at the College of Agriculture at the University of Illinois (1938-1939), editor of publications for the Illinois State Library (1939-1943), captain in the U.S. Army (1943-1946), librarian of the Quartermaster Technical Library in Fort Lee, Virginia (1946-1948), and librarian of the Institute of Labor and Industrial Relations at the University of Illinois (1948-1955). In 1955, he was appointed director of libraries of Southern Illinois University in Carbondale and Edwardsville, retiring in 1976.

McCoy was president of the Illinois Library Association in 1956 and was presented with the association's Award for Outstanding

Contribution to the Library Profession in 1961. In 1966-1967, he was president of the Association of College and Research Libraries.

McCoy is the author of two monumental compilations dealing with censorship: *Freedom of the Press; A Bibliography* (1968 and 1979). A third volume to update the work is in preparation. He was interim university librarian at the University of Georgia from 1978 to 1979, interim executive director of the Association of Research Libraries from 1980 to 1981, and interim librarian of Rutgers University from 1985 to 1986. He was appointed a member of the Illinois Center for the Book Committee in 1989.

McCRUM, BLANCHE P. (1887-1969) was born in Lexington, Virginia. She earned a library certificate from Drexel Institute in Philadelphia in 1913 and for the next five years worked at the Carnegie Library in Pittsburgh. She became assistant librarian of Washington and Lee University from 1918 until 1922, when she was appointed librarian. She filled that post until 1937, when she went on to become librarian of Wellesley College until 1947. Along the way, she attended Berkeley for a master's degree in library science under Sydney Mitchell and attended Boston University in 1930 for a bachelor's degree.

Based on her experience at Washington and Lee and on her observations elsewhere, Miss McCrum wrote a highly influential work, *An Estimate of Standards for a College Library* (1933), which was adopted as a text in a number of library schools for library administration courses.

Blanche McCrum was president of the Virginia Library Association for two years, from 1934 to 1936. She was a member of a planning committee that developed a landmark *Library Plan for Virginia*, which proposed certification for the state's future librarians, more state aid for school libraries, and an adequate state library building.

Miss McCrum's practical accomplishments at Washington and Lee were substantial: she was instrumental in developing a well-planned library use course, weekly play-readings in the library, an attractive browsing room, an area for manuscripts and special collections, open stacks, and an active friends of the library organization.

In 1937, Miss McCrum became librarian of Wellesley College, where she worked closely with a sympathetic and understanding president, Mildred H. McAfee. Off campus, she was president of the Association of College and Research Libraries in 1945-1946. A controversy with the ALA was solved by the appointment of an ACRL secretary.

Blanche McCrum was nearing sixty when she accepted an invitation from librarian of Congress Luther Evans to become a bibliographer in the Library of Congress' general reference and bibliography division. There she worked with Henry J. Dubester and Donald H. Mugridge in the production of a work of outstanding importance for historical research, *A Guide to the Study of the United States of America,* published by the Library of Congress in 1960. Her biographer, Betty Ruth Kondayan, concluded that Blanche McCrum was a major influence on academic librarianship: "She was a small giant in her own way."

MCDONOUGH, ROGER HENRY (1909-) was born in Trenton, New Jersey. He graduated from Rutgers University in 1934 and from Columbia's School of Library Service in 1936. He was named reference librarian at Rutgers in 1934 and was appointed director of the New Brunswick (New Jersey) Public Library in 1937. For four years, from 1942 to 1946, he served in the U.S. Army Air Force and was discharged with the rank of captain. He returned to the New Brunswick Public Library until 1947, at which time he became director of the State Library of the New Jersey Department of Education; in effect, he became the New Jersey state librarian. A new state library and archives building was completed and occupied in Trenton in 1965.

McDonough was president of the American Association of State Libraries from 1951 to 1952 and was president of the American

Library Association from 1968 to 1969. He has been a surveyor or consultant for the state libraries of Texas, New Hampshire, Connecticut, North Carolina, and Florida.

McGuire, Alice Rebecca Brooks (1902-1975) was born in Philadelphia and graduated from Smith College. She held library science degrees from Drexel, from Columbia, and from the University of Chicago (Ph.D., 1958). She was an important figure in the field of school librarianship for more than forty years. She was an instructor at Chicago's Graduate Library School from 1944 to 1949, librarian of an elementary school, a laboratory school librarian for the University of Texas in 1951, and a faculty member of the University of Texas Graduate School of Library Science until 1972. She frequently served as a speaker, consultant, and workshop director throughout the country from 1951 until her death in 1975. She received the Grolier Award in 1962 and served as president of the American Association of School Librarians from 1953 to 1954. She was editor of *Top of the News* from 1949 to 1950 and school and children's library editor for the *Wilson Library Bulletin* from 1950 to 1960.

Mearns, David Chambers (1899-1981) was born in Washington, D.C., and spent virtually all of his life in that city. He began his employment at the Library of Congress as a reference assistant in the order division in 1918. From 1920 to 1939, he was chief assistant in the reading rooms, and from 1939 to 1941, he was superintendent of the reading rooms. He became chief reference librarian in 1941 and director of the reference department in 1943. From 1949 to 1951, he was assistant librarian, and from 1951 to 1967, he was chief of the manuscripts division and chair of American history. He served as honorary consultant for the humanities from 1967 to 1981. Mearns specialized in studies of Abraham Lincoln in the course of his numerous publications.

Meehan, John Silva (1793-1867) was appointed librarian of Congress by President Andrew Jackson to replace George Watterson, who was fired for political reasons. Meehan held the position for thirty-two years. Under Meehan, access to the collections was further liberalized, and in 1840, a program of "international intellectual cooperation" was begun through exchanges of U.S. official publications with foreign governments. In a fire in 1851, the library lost 35,000 books, including half of the Jefferson collection.

Merrill, Julia Wright (1881-1961) was born in Chillicothe, Ohio, the daughter of the head of the Cincinnati Public Library. Julia enrolled in the Cincinnati Public Library training class in 1898 and was an assistant there until 1902. She earned a B.L.S. degree from the University of Illinois Library School in 1903. From 1903 to 1925, she held various positions with the Wisconsin Library Commission, the Cedar Rapids (Iowa) Public Library, the Cincinnati Public Library, and the Ohio State Library. From 1925 to 1946, she was on the American Library Association staff in Chicago, first as executive assistant in the library extension division and later as head of the information and advisory services. Merrill was chief of the public library division until her retirement. She also taught in several library school summer sessions and served as acting ALA executive secretary in 1944.

Merritt, Leroy Charles (1912-1970) was born in Milwaukee, Wisconsin, and graduated from the University of Wisconsin in 1935. He earned a doctoral degree from the University of Chicago Graduate Library School in 1942. He was librarian of Longwood College in Farmville, Virginia, from 1942 to 1946 and was on the faculty at the University of California School of Librarianship at Berkeley from 1946 to 1966. He became associate dean of the University School of Librarianship in Eugene, Oregon, in 1964 and was promoted to dean in 1966. He remained in that position until 1970. He was especially concerned with issues relating to censorship and was editor from 1962 to 1970 of the *Newsletter on Intellectual Freedom*. He was a past president of the Association of American Library Schools. Merritt served in the U.S. Army from 1944 to 1945 during World War II.

METCALF, KEYES DEWITT (1889-1983) was born in Elyria, Ohio, the seventeenth of eighteen children. In a career that spanned more than seventy-five years, he was one of the giants of the library profession. He worked in public and university library administration, planned more than 500 library buildings, served as a consultant for 200 institutions (many in foreign countries), and actively participated in the American Library Association and other professional organizations.

Metcalf's first library experience was as a student assistant for six years at the Oberlin College Library under Azariah Root, where he gained valuable training in collection development, use of space, library building design, and administration. He entered the New York Public Library School in 1911, working part-time at the information desk and as chief of the stacks, and received a diploma in 1915. In 1916-1917, he returned to Oberlin to serve as acting director of the college library. Afterward, he came back to the New York Public Library, where he remained for the next two decades. In 1928, he became chief of the reference department. In 1937, Metcalf accepted a position as director of the Harvard University Library and as college librarian. His major accomplishments at Harvard included creation of the Houghton Library in 1942 for rare books and manuscripts, formation of the New England Deposit Library for cooperative storage, the design of new stacks under the Harvard Yard, and, in 1949, creation of the Lamont Undergraduate Library.

While at Harvard, Metcalf served as executive secretary of the Association of Research Libraries from 1938 to 1941 and as president of the American Library Association from 1942 to 1943. After his retirement in 1955, he taught in the Rutgers and Columbia library schools and became a world traveler and consultant in Europe, Africa, Asia, Australia, New Zealand, and Latin America, and in forty-one states of the United States. He had a profound influence on library building design and directed the administrative experience of over one hundred librarians. He promoted and helped to develop the Farmington Plan for cooperative acquisition of foreign publications and extensive microphotographic reproduction of foreign newspapers and other materials.

Metcalf was a prolific writer. In 1947, he began publication of the *Harvard Library Bulletin*. His *Planning Academic and Research Library Buildings* (1965) became a standard work in its field. His autobiography, *Random Recollections of an Anachronism*, was published in 1980 and again in 1989.

MILAM, CARL HASTINGS (1884-1963) was born in Harper County, Kansas, and graduated from the University of Oklahoma in 1907. He received a certificate from the New York State Library School in 1908 and spent a year (1908-1909) as a cataloger at the Purdue University Library. From 1909 to 1913, he was an organizer for the Public Library Commission of Indiana. He left Indiana in 1913 to become director of the Birmingham (Alabama) Public Library. One of his important accomplishments there was to open a branch library for blacks. During World War I, he was active in the ALA Library War Service from 1917 to 1919, finally becoming general director.

Following the resignation of George Utley in 1920, Milam was appointed ALA secretary, a post that filled the major portion of his professional career for the next twenty-eight years. His main interests as executive secretary were library education, international library development, and federal support for libraries. Milam left the ALA position in 1948 to become director of the United Nations Library in New York. He retired at age sixty-five.

A lively controversy erupted in 1949 when Milam was nominated for ALA president. There was precedent for the nomination. Two of Milam's predecessors as ALA secretary, Chalmers Hadley and George Utley, had subsequently served as president. But a group of "young Turks" demanded a change of ALA leadership after Milam's long tenure. They nominated by petition and succeeded in electing a brash young Louisville, Kentucky, public librarian named Clarence "Skip" Graham as president, defeating Milam. Several years later, in 1954, Milam was named honorary member of the ALA.

As ALA executive secretary, Milam was notably successful as a fund raiser for the association, as a national and international leader in librarianship, and as a promoter of public library development and adult education programs in libraries.

MILCZEWSKI, MARION A. (1912-), a native of Saginaw, Michigan, graduated from the University of Michigan in 1936. He attended the University of Illinois and received B.S. and M.S. degrees in library science (1938-1940). He served variously as assistant to the ALA executive secretary, as director of the International Relations Office in Washington, D.C., and as director of the Southeast States Cooperative Library Survey. He was assistant librarian of the University of California at Berkeley and director of the University of Washington Libraries and held assignments abroad in Mexico, Colombia, Venezuela, and Brazil. He was a Fulbright scholar in England from 1954 to 1955. His published works include *Libraries of the Southeast* (1949) and a number of survey reports dealing with Latin American libraries.

MILLER, ROBERT A. (1907-1989) was director of libraries at Indiana University for thirty years before retiring in 1972. At Indiana, he supervised the building of the main library on the Bloomington campus and of the Lilly Library and coordinated an eight-campus library system. Earlier, from 1936 to 1942, Miller had been director of libraries at the University of Nebraska. He held degrees from the University of Iowa and Columbia University and a doctorate from the University of Chicago Graduate Library School.

MINTO, JOHN (1863-1935) was born in Scotland. His *Reference Books* (1929) made him the British counterpart of Kroeger, Mudge, and Winchell in America. Minto's first professional job, from 1902 to 1906, was as librarian of the Brighton Public Library. He returned to Scotland in 1906 to become librarian of the Society of Writers to the Signet, a law library in Edinburgh. Minto was a frequent lecturer on reference books, was an expert in cataloging, and was a British member of the committee that produced the Anglo-American catalog code of 1909.

MITCHELL, SYDNEY BANCROFT (1878-1951) was born in Montreal. After completing two degrees at McGill University (1901-1904), he went on to the New York State Library School at Albany for a B.L.S. degree in 1904, then returned to McGill for four years as a cataloger. He moved to California in 1908 and headed the Stanford University Library's order department until 1911. Going on to Berkeley, he remained at the University of California for the rest of his life, except for a year (1926-1927) of teaching library science at the University of Michigan.

Positions occupied by Mitchell at Berkeley were in succession: he was head of the library's accessions department from 1911 to 1919, associate university librarian from 1919 to 1926, and dean of the School of Librarianship from 1927 to 1946.

Mitchell's hobby was horticultural rather than bibliographical. He grew prize-winning iris and wrote about gardening and plant breeding. He was president of the California Library Association from 1938 to 1939 and president of the Horticultural Society from 1933 to 1934. The graduates of the California library school during his deanship were remarkably loyal to him and were highly successful in the library profession.

MOHRHARDT, FOSTER EDWARD (1907-   ) was born in Lansing, Michigan, the brother of Charles M. Mohrhardt, who became director of the Detroit Public Library. Foster graduated from Michigan State University in 1929 and from the Columbia School of

Library Service in 1930. Later, in 1933, he earned a master's degree from the University of Michigan. He was a student assistant at Michigan State and was in the New York Public Library's science and technology division in 1930. He worked at the University of Michigan from 1931 to 1933 and at the Colorado State College of Education at Greeley from 1933 to 1934. Returning to Ann Arbor, he assisted William Warner Bishop in preparing the list of *Books for Junior College Libraries* (1938). His next move was to Lexington, Virginia, where he was librarian of Washington and Lee University for eight years, starting in 1938. He had a period of military service during World War II.

In 1948, Mohrhardt succeeded Francis St. John as director of the Veterans Administration Library Service. In 1954, he followed Ralph R. Shaw as director of the U.S. Department of Agriculture Library. Starting in 1968, he became program officer of the Council of Library Resources.

Mohrhardt was president of the Virginia Library Association and in 1966 was president of the Association of Research Libraries. For the 1967-1968 term, he was president of the American Library Association.

MOON, ERIC (1923-) is a native of Yeovil, England, and attended the School of Librarianship at the Loughborough College of Further Education in England from 1947 to 1949. Before coming to the United States, he was an assistant at the Southampton Public Library (1939-1948), area librarian with the Hertfordshire County Library (1949-1951), district librarian for the Finckley Public Library (1951-1954), and deputy borough librarian and curator for the Brentford and Chizwick Public Library (1954-1956). He was head of technical processes at the Kensington Public Library from 1956 to 1958 and director of public library service and secretary of the public library board at St. Johns, Newfoundland, Canada, from 1958 to 1959. From 1959 to 1968, he was editor of the *Library Journal*. He has had an active role in library associations in the United States, England, and Canada, serving as president of the American Library Association in 1977-1978. He received the Joseph W. Lippincott Award in 1981. Earlier, from 1969 to 1978, he was president of Scarecrow Press. Moon has been a prolific writer on censorship and collection development.

MOORE, ANNE CARROLL (1871-1961) was born in Limerick, Maine, and graduated from Pratt Institute Library School in 1896. She was head of the children's department of the Pratt Institute Free Library from 1896 to 1906 and superintendent of work with children for the New York Public Library from 1906 to 1941. She was the author of a number of books for children and of publications to guide librarians who work with children. She was also a critic of children's books.

MORIARTY, JOHN HELENBECK (1903-1971) was born in Waterbury, Connecticut, and graduated from Columbia College in 1926. He subsequently earned two degrees (1934 and 1938) from the Columbia School of Library Service. In Waterbury, he served as a page in the public library while attending elementary school and high school. His first professional job was as librarian of the Cooper Union Institute of Technology from 1935 to 1939. In 1939, he became assistant to the director of libraries at Columbia and taught courses for the School of Library Service. He moved to the Library of Congress in 1941, first as chief of the accessions division and then as assistant director of the acquisition department. In 1944, Moriarty was appointed director of the Purdue University Library. During his stay in that position, the library's holdings grew from 200,000 to more than one million volumes between 1944 and 1970, and a strong system of departmental and school libraries was developed. Added responsibilities came to Moriarty in 1950 when he was appointed director of Purdue's Audio Visual Center.

Moriarty's concern for library education continued when he taught at summer sessions from 1950 to 1956 for the University of Illinois Library School. He played an active role in a number of professional organizations.

MORSCH, LUCILLE M. (1906-1972) was born in Sioux City, Iowa, and graduated from the University of Iowa in Iowa City in 1927. She began her library career during her freshman year in college as a student assistant in the catalog department at the university library. She received a fellowship for study at the Columbia School of Library Service, where she earned B.S. and M.S. degrees in 1929 and 1930. During the next ten years, she was employed in the New York Public Library's preparations division, as a cataloger at the University of Iowa (1930-1935), and as head of the catalog department at the Enoch Pratt Library in Baltimore (1935-1940). During several summers, she taught cataloging at Columbia. In 1940, she joined the Library of Congress as chief of the descriptive cataloging division. Foreign travel occupied her in 1949, when she was sent by the U.S. State Department and the Library of Congress on a ten-week trip through Latin America to visit ninety-nine libraries. In 1955, she attended an International Congress of Librarians in Brussels and visited many European libraries.

In 1951-1952, Miss Morsch served as chief of the general reference and bibliography division of the Library of Congress, and in 1953, she was appointed deputy chief assistant librarian of the Library of Congress.

Miss Morsch was long active in library associations. She became vice-president of the American Library Association in 1956 and was president in 1957-1958.

MORTON, ELIZABETH HOMAN (1903-) was born in Trinidad, British West Indies, and grew up in Saint John, New Brunswick. She graduated from Dalhousie University in 1926.

Miss Morton was on the staff of the Toronto Public Library for sixteen months doing cataloging and reference work. After an interim from 1928 to 1930, during which she was a librarian at

St. John Vocational School, she returned to the Toronto Public Library in 1931 as reference librarian and bibliographer until 1944.

From 1936 to 1943, she was secretary-treasurer of the Ontario Library Association. When the Canadian Library Council was incorporated in 1943, she became its secretary, after 1944, on a full-time basis. In 1946, the Canadian Library Association was founded, and Miss Morton served as its executive secretary from 1946 to 1968. Since 1946, she has also edited the CLA's official journal, *Canadian Library*. The *Canadian Index to Periodicals* has been published by the association since 1948. The CLA promoted establishment of the Canadian National Library, approved by the Parliament in 1952.

MORTON, FLORRINELL FRANCIS (1905-) was born in Pollock, Texas, and graduated from the University of California in 1925. She received a certificate in library science in 1927 and a master's degree in 1931. From 1927 to 1931, she was a cataloger at the North Texas State College Library at Denton. In 1931-1933, she was an instructor at the University of Illinois Library School. Her long tenure as a faculty member, and later as director of the Louisiana State University Library School, began in 1933 and continued until 1971. As an educator, Mrs. Morton has shown particular concern for establishing standards in education for school librarianship and for school library accreditation.

In professional organizations, Mrs. Morton has served as president of the Southwestern Library Association (1960-1962), as president of the Louisiana Library Association (1941-1942), as president of the Association of American Library Schools (1946-1947), and as president of the American Library Association 1961-1962).

MUDGE, ISADORE GILBERT (1875-1957) was born in Brooklyn, New York. She was America's foremost reference librarian and for many years was the author of the standard *Guide to*

Reference Books. She graduated from Cornell University in 1897. The following year, she enrolled at the New York State Library School, directed by Melvil Dewey, and earned a bachelor of library science degree with distinction in 1900. On Dewey's recommendation, she joined another Dewey disciple, Katharine Lucinda Sharp, at the University of Illinois in 1900 as head of the reference department. In 1903, she resigned from Illinois to become librarian of Bryn Mawr College until 1908. The next three years were filled with various activities, including part-time teaching at the Simmons College Library School in Boston until 1911, when Miss Mudge accepted a position as gifts and exchanges librarian at Columbia University. A few months later, she was appointed reference librarian, a position in which she remained until her retirement in 1941, after thirty years.

At Columbia, Miss Mudge stressed the development of an outstanding reference collection and its services. She also took over the *Guide to Reference Books*, the undisputed leader among reference guides originally compiled by Alice Bertha Kroeger. Four editions of the *Guide* were published from 1917 to 1936, with intervening supplements. In addition, Miss Mudge was on the faculty of the Columbia School of Library Service, where she served as associate professor of bibliography from 1927 to 1938.

Miss Mudge's companion and collaborator for several decades was Minnie Earl Sears, head of the Columbia Library cataloging department.

MUMFORD, LAWRENCE QUINCY (1903-1982) was born in Ayden, North Carolina. He graduated from Duke University in 1925 and received an M.A. degree in 1928. He was a student assistant at the Duke library for three years and later became head of the circulation department. This was followed by his appointment as acting chief of reference and circulation.

While studying at the School of Library Service at Columbia for a B.S. degree, Mumford held a student assistantship at the university library. Afterward, he filled a number of positions at the New York Public Library from 1929 to 1945. He was given a leave of absence from 1940 to 1942 to reorganize the processing division of the Library of Congress. From 1950 to 1954, Mumford was director of the Cleveland Public Library, one of the largest public library systems in the United States.

In 1954, Mumford was nominated by President Eisenhower as librarian of Congress. Among the highlights of Mumford's two decades as librarian was completion of the James Madison Memorial Building, for which funds had been appropriated in 1971. The first Library of Congress building, named the Thomas Jefferson Building, under Spofford, was occupied in 1897. The second, called the Annex and subsequently renamed the John Adams Building, under Putnam, was completed in 1939. During Mumford's twenty years as librarian, the library's collections more than doubled, and annual expenditures increased several times over. He traveled extensively in many foreign countries to promote the library's worldwide interests. Mumford's final two years as librarian were handicapped by poor health, but he continued in office until 1974.

In professional organizations, Mumford was president of the Ohio Library Association from 1947 to 1948, vice-president of the American Library Association from 1953 to 1954, and president of the ALA from 1954 to 1955.

In addition to his survey of the Library of Congress technical services, Mumford assisted in surveying the Army Medical Library, the Columbia University Library, and the American Library in Paris.

MUNN, RALPH (1894-1975) was born in Aurora, Illinois. He graduated from the University of Denver with a B.A. in 1916 and an LL.B. in 1917. From 1917 to 1919, he served with the U.S. Army in France and then entered the New York State Library School at Albany, where he received a B.L.S. in 1921. His first professional position was as a reference librarian at the Seattle Public Library from 1921 to 1926. From here, he moved to become librarian of the Flint (Michigan) Public Library, and in 1928, he became director of the Carnegie Library of Pittsburgh until his retirement in 1964. Munn also served as dean of the Carnegie Institute of Technology from 1928 to 1962.

In 1934, Munn undertook a four-month tour to study the library situation in Australia and New Zealand. His far-reaching report and recommendations led to his being called the "father of the modern library movement" in those countries. Later, in 1950, he was a delegate to the United Nations conference in Malmo, Sweden, to determine the needs of libraries throughout the world.

Munn was president of the American Library Association in 1939-1940. He received the Pennsylvania Library Association's first Distinguished Service Award in 1959.

MUNTHE, WILHELM (1883-1965) was librarian of the University of Oslo for many years and president of the International Federation of Library Associations from 1947 to 1951. He traveled extensively in Europe and the United States. In 1936, he reported his observations and opinions, based on visits to thirty-six states and Canada, in a widely read book, *American Librarianship from a European Angle.*

NAUDÉ, GABRIEL (1600-1653) was born in Paris and graduated from the University of Paris. He spent most of his life as a practicing librarian and scholar. In the employ of Cardinal Mazarin, he traveled widely to collect a library of 40,000 volumes and many manuscripts. Political disorders in 1652 led to the break up and dispersal of the Mazarin library. After the cardinal's death, it was reconstructed. Naudé's treatise on librarianship, published in 1644, is regarded as a classic; it deals with the procurement and arrangement of books, library management, classification, library buildings, and other matters.

NELSON, CHARLES ALEXANDER (1839-1933) was born in Calais, Maine. He graduated from Harvard College in 1860 and received a master's degree from Harvard in 1863.

Nelson was preeminent as a bibliographer. He prepared a catalog of the Astor Library (1886-1888), a catalog of the Avery Architectural Library (1895), and other works. He was at the Newberry Library from 1891 to 1893. He was the first librarian of the Howard Memorial Library at New Orleans (1888-1891). In 1893, he was appointed deputy librarian of Columbia University and remained there until his retirement in 1909.

NICHOLSON, EDWARD WILLIAMS BYRON (1849-1912) graduated from Oxford University's Trinity College in 1874. Until 1882, he was librarian of the London Institution, and for the next thirty years, he was librarian of the Oxford University Library. His initiative led to the founding of the British Library Association in 1877, one year after the founding of the American Library Association. He was editor of the transactions and proceedings of the first conference of British librarians.

OLCOTT, FRANCES JENKINS (1872-1963) was born in Paris, France, and graduated from the New York State Library School in 1896. She was assistant librarian of the Brooklyn Public Library from 1897 to 1898 and then became head of the children's department of the Carnegie Library of Pittsburgh from 1900 to 1911. Her writings and library association activities brought attention to the children's library movement. Following her stay in Pittsburgh, she devoted full time to writing, producing many anthologies of fairy tales, stories, biographies, and poems for children, some of which have been revised and reprinted.

ORAM, ROBERT W. (1922-) was born in Warsaw, Indiana. He graduated from the University of Toledo in 1949 and from the University of Illinois Library School in 1950. He was assistant to the librarian of the University of Missouri in Columbia from 1950 to 1956 and circulation librarian at the University of Illinois in Urbana from 1956 to 1967. In 1968, he was promoted to be director of public service departments at the University of Illinois, and he held this position until 1971. He was associate university librarian from 1971 to 1979 and acting university librarian from 1975 to 1976. Oram became director of the Southern Methodist University libraries in 1979 and retired in 1989. He is a leader in the national friends of libraries movement. Oram served with the U.S. Army, European Theater of Operations, from 1942 to 1946.

ORNE, JERROLD (1911-) was born in St. Paul, Minnesota, and graduated from the University of Minnesota with bachelor's and master's degrees in languages and literature. He spent a year in Paris at the Sorbonne, after which he went to the University of Chicago for a Ph.D. in languages. There he met Louis R. Wilson, who urged him to obtain a library science degree. For that purpose, he returned to the University of Minnesota, receiving a bachelor's degree in library science in 1939. A fellowship enabled him to spend a year at the Library of Congress under Archibald MacLeish, helping to develop collections in romance languages and library science.

In 1941, Orne was appointed librarian of Knox College, where he remained until drafted into the navy in 1943. He was sent to San Francisco to help establish a reference library for the United Nations Conference on International Organization. In 1944, he proceeded to Washington, assigned to the navy's Office of Research and Inventions to organize a large collection of navy research reports. Still in Washington, he then served as director of the Office of Technical Services of the Library Division at the U.S. Department of Commerce. Several academic appointments followed. From 1945 to 1951, he was director of the Washington University Library in St. Louis. In 1951, he was appointed director of the Air University Library in Alabama, a post for which he was well suited due to his military experience. He knew how to deal with military personnel and was aided by able staff members such as Robert Delzell and Mike Field. Under his guidance, the Air University Library was transformed into a first-class research institution in its field. The next step for Orne was appointment as librarian of the University of North Carolina at Chapel Hill in 1957. During that period, a new undergraduate library was built.

Orne is a dynamic personality who frequently has engaged in controversies. He retired from administrative duties in 1973 to join the library school faculty at Chapel Hill. His teaching career continued for three years until he retired in 1976.

Orne's major achievements include training a number of outstanding leaders for the library profession, developing collections, planning library buildings, working to establish library standards in cooperation with the American Standards Association, and writing more than 100 articles, reviews, and monographs. Orne's contributions to academic librarianship were recognized by the American Library Association through his receipt of the Lippincott Award. A *festschrift* was published by Bowker in 1977, *Academic Libraries in the Year 2000; Essays Honoring Jerrold Orne.*

OTUKEN, ADNAN (1911-   ), director of the Turkish National Library, was born in Manastir, Turkey. He graduated from the University of Istanbul and then went to Germany from 1935 to 1939 to complete a degree in library science at the Prussian State Library in Berlin. While in Germany, he gained practical experience at the Deutsch Bucherei in Leipzig. After his return to Turkey, Otuken was made director of publications of the Ministry of Education, a post that he filled for five years. In 1946, he was assigned by the ministry to the task of founding the Turkish National Library in Ankara. The library was charged with collecting all copyright copies of Turkish books, newspapers, and periodicals. Since 1951, the library has been responsible for publishing the Turkish national bibliography and a monthly library bulletin. Otuken teaches at the University of Ankara library school and for a number of years has talked about books over the Ankara radio station. He is the author of the standard Turkish manual of library science and bibliography and has traveled widely in Western Europe and the United States to visit libraries.

PALTSITS, VICTOR HUGO (1867-1952), bibliographer, librarian, and historian, was born in New York City and had limited formal education. In 1888, he joined the staff of the Lenox Library. After the establishment of the New York Public Library in 1895, he became assistant librarian under John Shaw Billings. In 1907, Paltsits was appointed New York state historian for a four-year term. From 1911 to 1928, he was associated both full- and part-time with the historian I. N. Phelps Stokes. In 1914, he returned to the New York Public Library as its first keeper of manuscripts. Two years later, he became chief of the American history division, a position that he held until his retirement in 1941.

Paltsits was a prolific writer who produced a steady stream of published works, including numerous biographical sketches. He was a founding member of the Bibliographical Society of America and its first president, in 1938-1939. He also helped to found the American Military History Foundation, the History of Science Society, and the Society of American Archivists.

PANIZZI, SIR ANTHONY (1797-1879) was born in Brescello, a duchy of Modena, Italy. He was arrested for conspiring against the Modena government but escaped prison and a death sentence and fled to London. The influence of the chancellor of the British Museum, Henry Peter Brougham, led to Panizzi's appointment as assistant librarian in that institution in 1831. For a time, he followed certain interests in Italian literature and worked on a manuscript catalog of the British Museum. In 1837, he was promoted to be keeper of the printed books. Space was extremely limited, and Panizzi's plan led to the opening of a new building in 1857. Panizzi became principal librarian in 1856, succeeding Sir Henry Ellis. One of the major improvements during his administration was stricter enforcement of the copyright act. Numerous important collections were added to the museum's holdings during the course of his stay. Panizzi resigned his position in June 1866. He was knighted by Queen Victoria in 1869.

Panizzi had three principles of administration in managing the British Museum: it was not a show, but an institution for the diffusion of culture; it was a department of the civil service and should be conducted in the spirit of other public departments; and it should be managed with the utmost possible liberality.

A lifetime concern for Panizzi was the movement for the liberation of Italy.

PARGELLIS, STANLEY (1898-1968), the fifth librarian of the Newberry Library, was born in Toledo, Ohio. He graduated from the University of Nevada in 1918 and was a Rhodes scholar at Oxford, where he earned B.A. and M.A. degrees. He received a Ph.D. from Yale in 1929. From 1923 to 1942, he taught history at the California Institute of Technology and at Yale University.

In 1942, Pargellis began twenty years as librarian of the Newberry Library. He remained somewhat apart from the technical aspects of librarianship while maintaining close relationships with many members of the profession. His major published work was the *Bibliography of British History: the Eighteenth Century, 1714-1789* (1951). Pargellis spent a year after his retirement in Canberra, Australia, to advise the Commonwealth National Library.

Parker, Ralph Halstead (1909-   ) was born in Bertram, Texas. He graduated from the University of Texas in 1930 and received a Ph.D. degree from the University of Chicago Graduate Library School in 1937. He began his library career at the University of Texas, first as a loan librarian from 1930 to 1935, then as an assistant archivist from 1935 to 1936. From 1936 to 1937, he was a research assistant at the University of Chicago.

He was the librarian of Pomona College from 1937 to 1940 and director of libraries at the University of Georgia from 1940 to 1947. After military service in World War II, he became librarian of the University of Missouri from 1947 to 1969.

Parker was president of the Missouri Library Association in 1951-1952. He is widely known as an expert in data processing and machine records. He is the author of *Library Applications of Punched Cards* (1952).

Piercy, Esther June (1905-1967) was born in Los Angeles and graduated from the University of Idaho in 1930. She received a B.S. degree from the University of Illinois Library School in 1932. Her professional positions included ten years as a cataloger at the University of New Mexico (1934-1944) and as assistant librarian of the Worcester (Massachusetts) Public Library. From 1948 until her death, she was chief of processing at the Enoch Pratt Free Library in Baltimore. Miss Piercy was editor of the *Journal of Cataloging and Classification* from 1950 to 1956 and of *Library Resources and Technical Services* from 1957 to 1967. She was awarded the Margaret Mann Cataloging Medal.

Plummer, Mary Wright (1856-1916) was a native of Richmond, Indiana, and the daughter of Quaker parents. Her library career began in 1887 when she joined Melvil Dewey's first class at Columbia's School of Library Economy. She spent two years, 1888 to 1890, as a cataloger at the St. Louis Public Library. After a summer in Europe, she went to Pratt Institute Free Library to be an administrative assistant and to help conduct a training class for beginning librarians. The class developed into a library school, and in 1895, Miss Plummer became not only its head, but also director of the Pratt Library. The two positions were separated in 1904 in order for her to give full time to operating the school. In 1911, she became the first principal of the New York Public Library School, where she remained until her death in 1916.

Miss Plummer was the second woman president of the American Library Association, from 1915 to 1916. Previously, she had been president of the New York Library Club (1896-1897 and 1913-1914) and president of the New York Library Association (1906). She was a U.S. delegate to the International Library Congress in Paris in 1900 and was in charge of the ALA exhibit at the Paris Exposition. During several trips to Europe, she visited a number of libraries in Italy, Germany, and France. She always showed a special concern for the role of women in librarianship, perhaps inspired by Melvil Dewey's insistence on admitting women to the first library school at Columbia.

POOLE, WILLIAM FREDERICK (1821-1894) was born in Salem, Massachusetts, and graduated from Yale College in 1848. In his junior year, he was assistant to librarian John Edwards. After graduation, he served for four years as librarian of the Boston Mercantile Library Association. From 1856 to 1869, he was librarian of the Boston Athenaeum, and from 1871 to 1873, he was head of the Cincinnati Public Library. In 1874, Poole was appointed the first librarian of the Chicago Public Library. This institution became the country's largest circulating library while under his administration. His last position was as organizer and librarian of the Newberry Library, from 1887 to 1894.

Poole was president of the American Historical Association in 1888, was one of the organizers of the American Library Association in 1876, served as ALA president in 1885-1887, and was vice-president of the International Conference of Librarians in London in 1877. Poole is most famous among librarians for his *Poole's Index to Periodical Literature* (1853).

Powell, Benjamin Edward (1905-1981) was born in Sunbury, North Carolina. He graduated from Duke University and from the Columbia School of Library Service (1926-1930). He received a doctoral degree from the University of Chicago Graduate Library School in 1946. He began his professional career as an assistant at the Duke library from 1927 to 1929. From 1930 to 1937, he was a reference librarian and supervisor of circulation at Duke. From 1937 to 1946, he served as librarian of the University of Missouri and then was recalled to become librarian of Duke in 1946.

Powell was president of the Missouri Library Association in 1938-1939, president of the Association of College and Reference Libraries in 1948-1949, and president of the American Library Association in 1960-1961.

Powell, Lawrence Clark (1906-   ) was born in Washington, D.C., but his family moved to southern California in 1911. His personality was described as "a compulsive extroverted ham" when he was admitted to Occidental College in 1924. As a student, he was active in campus politics, journalism, dramatics, and debating. He made a round-the-world cruise, playing in a ship's orchestra between his freshman and sophomore years. After graduation in 1929, he worked for a time in a Pasadena bookstore and then went to France to attend the University of Dijon, where he completed a doctoral degree in American literature. After returning to the United States, Powell was employed at Jacob Zeitlin's bookstore, where he became familiar with the antiquarian book trade. Althea Warren, director of the Los Angeles Public Library, encouraged him to become a librarian. He entered the Berkeley Library School in 1936. Thereafter, he was given a temporary appointment on the Los Angeles Public Library staff and then a beginning library position at UCLA under director John E. Goodwin. After declining a position as director of the Northwestern University Libraries, Powell was appointed university librarian and director of the Clark Library at UCLA in 1944. Under Powell, the UCLA Library experienced a phenomenal growth in the number of volumes, in the book budget, and in the size of the staff.

Powell retired as university librarian in 1961 to serve for the next six years as dean of the new UCLA Library School. He also retained his position as head of the Clark Library. In 1971, he moved to the University of Arizona at Tucson to become professor-in-residence, without clearly defined duties.

Powell had missionary zeal in his belief in the importance of books. His personality has been described as "an attractive symbolic leader, earthy, salty, brash westerner, defender of intellectual freedom, a world traveler, excellent speaker, and extrovert," all contrary to the stereotyped image of a professional librarian. As Powell saw himself, he irked people because of a "personal, autobiographical, egocentric, didactic, flamboyant, hyperbolic manner." His autobiography, *Fortune and Friendship*, was published in 1968.

Powell recruited a number of leading figures into the library world: Robert Vosper, Andrew Horn, Page Ackerman, and many others. His prolific, influential writings, such as *A Passion for Books* (1959) and *Books in My Baggage* (1960), are widely read. In 1949-1950, he was president of the California Library Association, and he took the lead in creating the University of California Library Council.

POWER, EFFIE LOUISE (1873-1969), born in Conneautville, Pennsylvania, received a diploma from the Training School for Children's Libraries at the Carnegie Library of Pittsburgh. She won fame for her many contributions to library service for children. She spent several periods at the Cleveland Public Library, first as an apprentice under William Howard Brett (1895), and from 1920 to 1937 as director of work with children. From 1903 to 1908, she taught courses in library use and in children's literature at the City Normal School in Cleveland. Until 1929, she taught courses at Western Reserve University, specializing in work with children and storytelling.

After Miss Power retired from the Cleveland Public Library in 1937, she joined the faculty of the School of Library Service at Columbia University, where she remained until 1939. While at Cleveland, she introduced, in 1926, the book caravan, a mobile library that was the forerunner of the modern bookmobile. In professional organizations, she was the president of the library department of the National Education Association and chairman of the children's section of the ALA in 1912-1913 and in 1929-1930.

PRICE, MILES OSCAR (1890-1968), born in Plymouth, Indiana, was librarian of the Columbia University Law School from 1929 to 1961. Because of his exceptional influence on law librarianship, he was called dean of law librarians. He received a B.S. degree from the University of Chicago in 1914, working his way through college as a library assistant. For eight years, he served as a department chief at the University of Illinois Library. He received a B.L.S. degree from the Illinois Library School in 1922. From 1922 to 1929, he was librarian of the U.S. Patent Office Library in Washington, D.C. In 1929, he succeeded Frederick C. Hicks as librarian of the Columbia Law School. While in that position, he received an LL.B. degree in 1938, was admitted to the New York bar in 1940, and was appointed professor of law at Columbia in 1956.

Price was president of the District of Columbia Library Association in 1924-1925 and president of the American Association of Law Libraries in 1945-1946. From 1937 to 1961, he taught a course in legal bibliography and law library administration at the Columbia School of Library Service.

PURDY, GEORGE FLINT (1905-1969) was born in Mason City, Iowa, and graduated from Iowa State Teachers College in 1925. He won his first library degree from the Columbia School of Library Service in 1933 and went on to receive a Ph.D. from the University of Chicago Graduate Library School in 1936. He spent the remainder of his career — thirty-three years — as director of the Wayne State University Library in Detroit.

Purdy was president of the ALA library education division from 1949 to 1950, president of the Michigan Library Association, and chairman of the board of directors of the Center for Research Libraries.

PUTNAM, HERBERT (1861-1955) was a native of New York and the son of George Palmer Putnam. He graduated from Harvard and Columbia Law School. His first professional position as a librarian was as head of the Minneapolis Athenaeum and later as head of its successor, the Minneapolis Public Library. In 1895, Putnam became director of the Boston Public Library. He remained in that position until 1899, when he was appointed librarian of Congress by nomination of President McKinley. One of Putnam's first acts was to arrange for a new and vastly revised classification scheme. This resulted in the creation of the Library of Congress classification, designed for libraries of great size. Also initiated were the practice of interlibrary loans and the sale to other libraries of cards printed by the Library of Congress. The Legislative Reference Service was established in 1915. Emphasis was placed on building the largest collection of Orientalia outside the East. With a grant from John D. Rockefeller in 1927, the National Union Catalog was begun. In 1930, a major addition to the library's rare-book holdings was the acquisition of the Vallbehr collection of incunabula. After forty years of directing the Library of Congress, Putnam retired in 1939 and died in 1955 at the age of ninety-four.

QUIGLEY, MARGERY CLOSEY (1886-1968) was born in Los Angeles and graduated from Vassar College in 1908. She began her library career at the St. Louis Public Library from 1909 to 1918. In 1918, she was appointed librarian of the Endicott (New York) Public Library, and she attended the New York State Library School, from which she received a certificate in 1923. In 1924-1925, she served as president of the New York Library Association. From 1925 to 1927, she was a branch librarian at the Washington (D.C.) Public Library, from which she moved on to become librarian of the Montclair Public Library from 1927 to 1956. One of her innovations at Montclair was designing electronic data processing techniques for library procedures. In 1955, Miss Quigley was able to obtain a new main library building for Montclair, widely admired for its pioneering architectural features. For more than twenty years she taught at Columbia and at other library schools.

RANGANATHAN, S. R. (1892-1972) has been described correctly as the "father of library science in India." He was National Research Professor in Library Science in India from 1965 until his death at age eighty-one in 1972. His previous positions were as university librarian and professor of library science at Benares Hindu University (1945-1947), as professor of library science at the University of Delhi (1947-1955), and as professor of the documentation research and training centre at Bangalore (1962-1964). He was the creator of the colon classification, which some critics suggest is comparable in importance to Melvil Dewey's invention of the decimal classification.

Ranganathan was a pioneer in applying scientific methods to the study of librarianship. Among his numerous works are *The Five Laws of Library Science* (1931), *Colon Classification* (1933), *Classified Catalogue Code* (1934), and *Library Administration* (1935). An International Conference on Ranganathan was held in 1985 in Delhi to discuss his philosophy and other aspects of his teachings. Ranganathan received the ALA Margaret Mann Citation for 1970.

RATHBONE, JOSEPHINE ADAMS (1864-1941) was born in Jamestown, New York. After attending Wellesley College and the University of Michigan (1882-1885), she enrolled in the New York State Library School and received a B.L.S. degree in 1893. She worked for a year, 1892-1893, as assistant librarian of the Diocesan Lending Library at the All Saints Cathedral in Albany. For the next forty-five years, she was associated with the Pratt Institute, founded in Brooklyn in 1887. In 1895, she was appointed assistant to Mary Wright Plummer and taught at the Pratt Library School. In 1911, she was placed in direct charge of the school.

Miss Rathbone was active in professional organizations. She was founder of the Association of American Library Schools in 1915 and served as its president for two terms, 1920-1921 and 1927-1928. A greater honor came when she was elected president of the American Library Association in 1931-1932. She was also president of the New York Library Club from 1918 to 1919 and president of the Long Island Library Association from 1912 to 1913.

READY, WILLIAM B. (1914-1981) was born in Cardiff, Wales. He held degrees from the University of Wales, from Oxford University, from the University of Manitoba, from the University of Western Ontario, and from Rutgers University. During World War II, he was with the British Army from 1939 to 1945. His first library experience was as an assistant in the Cardiff Public Library (1931-1939). After coming to the United States in 1948, he was a teaching fellow at the University of Minnesota (1948-1950), an instructor at the University of California Graduate Library School (1950-1951), assistant director of acquisitions for the Stanford University Library (1951-1956), librarian of Marquette University (1956-1963), librarian of Sacred Heart University in Connecticut (1963-1966), and librarian of McMaster University in Hamilton, Ontario (1966-1981). Ready won the Atlantic Monthly Award in 1948, the Clarence Day Award in 1961, and the Thomas More Award in 1962.

Ready's autobiography, *Files on Parade*, was published in 1982. A department of McMaster University has been named the William Ready Division of Archives and Research Collections.

REED, SARAH REBECCA (1914-1978) was born in Warren, Illinois, and graduated from Cornell College in 1936. She received library science degrees from the University of Illinois (1945) and the University of Chicago (1946). She began her library career as a library school librarian from 1936 to 1942 and as a supervisor of induction training at the University of Chicago from 1946 to 1952. She moved on to teaching and administrative positions in graduate library schools at the University of Denver, at the University of North Carolina, at Florida State University, at the University of Alberta, at Indiana University, and at Emporia State. She served as executive secretary of the ALA library education division, as secretary of the ALA committee on accreditation (1960-1963), and as library education specialist at the U.S. Office of Education. In 1968, she received the Beta Phi Mu Award for distinguished service to education for librarianship.

Miss Reed was in an accident on Lake Pomona in Kansas in 1978 and drowned after being thrown from an overturned boat.

RICE, PAUL NORTH (1888-1967), a native of Lowell, Massachusetts, graduated from Wesleyan University in 1910 and from the New York State Library School in Albany in 1913. From 1911 to 1913, he was assistant reference librarian of Ohio State University. He filled several positions in the reference department of the New York Public Library: he was a reference assistant at the information desk (1914-1916), chief of stacks (1916-1917), chief of the accessions division and later chief of the preparation division

(1920-1927), and chief of the reference department (1938-1953), succeeding Keyes D. Metcalf. During World War I, from 1917 to 1919, he served in the U.S. Army. From 1927 to 1936, he was head librarian of the Dayton (Ohio) Public Library, and from 1936 to 1937, he was director of libraries at New York University. After his retirement from the New York Public Library in 1953, Rice became librarian of Wesleyan University from 1953 to 1956, succeeding Fremont Rider.

Rice was active in various library organizations, serving as president of the Ohio Library Association from 1930 to 1931, as president of the New York Library Association from 1939 to 1940, and as president of the American Library Association from 1947 to 1948. From 1942 to 1945, he was executive secretary of the Association of Research Libraries, during which time he actively promoted the Farmington Plan and publication of the Library of Congress catalog in book form.

RICHARDS, JOHN STEWART (1892-1979) was born in Chicago and graduated from the University of Washington School of Librarianship in 1916. His first professional job was as librarian of the Marshfield Public Library in southwestern Oregon. In 1918-1919, he was active in the ALA war service program. After a year's study, 1919-1920, at the New York State Library School in Albany, he became librarian of Idaho Technical Institute at Pocatello until 1923. From 1923 to 1929, he was librarian of the Washington State Normal School in Ellenberg. Moving to Berkeley, he was circulation librarian of the University of California from 1926 to 1929. While there, he received a master's degree from the School of Librarianship in 1932 and served as assistant librarian from 1929 to 1934. From 1934 to 1941, he was an executive assistant at the University of Washington Library and associate librarian from 1941 to 1942. In April 1942, Richards succeeded Judson T. Jennings as librarian of the Seattle Public Library.

For the 1955-1956 term, Richards followed L. Quincy Mumford as president of the American Library Association.

RICHARDSON, ERNEST CUSHING (1860-1939) was a native of Woburn, Massachusetts, and a graduate of Amherst College and the Hartford Theological Seminary. He began his long career in librarianship as a student assistant at Amherst in his senior year. For six years, he was librarian of the Hartford Seminary. In 1890, he became librarian and professor of bibliography at the College of New Jersey, later Princeton University. He remained at Princeton in various capacities until 1925. From 1925 until his death at age seventy-nine, he served as a consultant in bibliography and research at the Library of Congress. He was president of the American Library Association in 1904-1905.

Richardson's scholarly interests were revealed in a number of pioneer works concerning library history, notably, *Biblical Libraries, The Beginnings of Libraries, Some Old Egyptian Libraries,* and *The Medieval Library.* Some controversy arose over Richardson's translation of "scribe" as "librarian" and "house of writing" to mean "library" in his writing about ancient libraries. In the modern sense, these were probably erroneous.

At the Library of Congress, Richardson strongly promoted the development of the National Union Catalog. By 1932, under Richardson's direction, the catalog had located seven million titles with nine million copies in American libraries. Also, 4,884 special collections were located in American libraries.

Richardson also wrote *Classification, Theoretical and Practical,* which was first published in 1901. This scheme was adopted by the Princeton Library. At Princeton, he was among the first in the country to purchase Library of Congress printed cards, evidence of his strong belief in cooperative cataloging.

RIDER, FREMONT (1885-1962) was born in Trenton, New Jersey. He graduated from Syracuse University in 1905 and attended the New York State Library School in Albany for a year. From 1906 to 1933, he had a varied career as a writer, a publisher, and a printer. In 1933, he was appointed librarian of Wesleyan University in Middletown, Connecticut. During his twenty years at Wesleyan, Rider established an active friends of the library organization, began printing catalog cards, and developed microcards for miniscule recording of information. Rider's most famous work was *The Scholar and the Future of the Research Library* (1944), dealing with problems caused by the rapid growth of library collections.

RODEN, CARL BISMARCK (1871-1956) was born in Kansas City, Missouri. He obtained his first taste of library work at age fifteen when he was a page at the Chicago Public Library. This was the start of sixty-four years in that institution. He progressed from assistant cataloger to chief of the catalog division in 1908. Finally, in 1918, he became librarian, a position that he held for thirty-two years. Under his direction, the library emphasized the collecting of Chicago history, of Americana, and of early printing. Its total holdings grew to over 2.5 million volumes by 1950, when Roden retired.

Roden held a number of offices in professional organizations: he was president of the Bibliographical Society of America (1917-1918), president of the Illinois Library Association (1905-1906), president of the Chicago Library Club (1899-1900), and president of the American Library Association (1927-1928).

ROGERS, FRANK BRADWAY (1914-   ) was born in Norwood, Ohio, and graduated from Yale in 1936. He received an M.D. degree from Ohio State University in 1942 and an M.S. in library science from the Columbia School of Library Service in 1949. From 1949 to 1963, Rogers served as director of the National Library of Medicine in Bethesda, Maryland. In 1962-1963, he was also president of the Medical Library Association. He served as honorary vice-president of the International Congress of Medical Librarianship in London in 1953. In 1961, he received an award from the Medical Library Association for his outstanding contributions to medical librarianship. The American Library Association presented him with the Melvil Dewey Medal in 1963.

Rogers became librarian of the University of Colorado Medical Center in 1963.

ROGERS, RUTHERFORD DAVID (1915-1988) was born in Jesup, Iowa. He graduated from the University of Northern Iowa in 1936 and from the Columbia School of Library Service in 1937. He began his professional career as an assistant at the New York Public Library from 1937 to 1938. He became a reference librarian at Columbia College Library at Columbia University in 1938 and held that position until 1941, when he was promoted to acting librarian (1941-1942), and finally to librarian (1942-1945). He was the director of the Grosvenor Library in Buffalo, New York (1948-1952), director of the Rochester Public Library (1952-1954), chief of the personnel office at the New York Public Library (1954-1955), chief of the reference department at the New York Public Library (1955-1957), deputy librarian of Congress (1957-1964), director of libraries at Stanford University (1964-1969), and librarian of Yale University (1969-1985). He was president of the Association of Research Libraries in 1967-1968. Rogers is coauthor with David C. Weber of a standard work, *University Library Administration* (1971). During World War II, from 1942 to 1946, Rogers served with the Air Transport Command, USAAF.

ROOT, AZARIAH SMITH (1862-1927) was born in Middlefield, Massachusetts. He received a bachelor's degree in 1884 and a master's degree in 1887 from Oberlin College. He was a student of law at Boston University from 1884 to 1885 and at Harvard Law School from 1886 to 1887. He attended the University of Göttingen in 1898-1899. He was appointed librarian of Oberlin College and professor of bibliography in 1887 and remained in that position for the remainder of his career.

ROTHROCK, MARY UTOPIA (1890-1976) was born in Trenton, Tennessee, and graduated with B.S. and M.S. degrees from Vanderbilt University (1911-1912). She earned a B.L.S. degree from the New York State Library School at Albany in 1922. Her first professional position was as head of the circulation department at Cossitt Library in Memphis (1914-1916). In 1916, she became librarian at the Lawson McGhee Library in Knoxville and served in that position until 1934. During her tenure at Knoxville, a strong public library was developed for the city, along with a branch system to serve the city and county. In 1934, she became supervisor of library services for the Tennessee Valley Authority (TVA), a post that she held until 1948. From 1949 to 1955, she was librarian of Knox County, Tennessee. For three years she was a library consultant to TVA.

Miss Rothrock was exceptionally involved in the work of various library organizations. She was a founder of the Southeastern Library Association (SELA) and served as its first president from 1922 to 1924. She was twice president of the Tennessee Library Association, in 1919-1920 and again in 1927-1928. She was a member of numerous ALA committees and served as vice-president in 1945-1946. From 1946 to 1947, she was president of the American Library Association. She received the ALA's first Lippincott Award in 1938 for her "outstanding contribution to librarianship. Her will left $10,000 to the SELA for a biennial award and a bequest of $285,000 to the McClung historical collection of the Knoxville–Knox County Public Library.

RUSH, CHARLES EVERETT (1885-1958) was born near Fairmont, Indiana, and graduated in 1905 from Earlham College. He worked as an assistant at the college library and received a B.L.S. degree from the New York State Library School in 1908. While preparing for a library career, he was an assistant at the Newark (New Jersey) Public Library. After his stay in Albany, Rush served as librarian of the Jackson (Michigan) Public Library, of the St. Joseph (Missouri) Public Library (1910-1916), and of the Des Moines (Iowa) Public Library (1916-1917). In 1917, he became director of a larger library system, the Indianapolis Public Library. He remained here until 1928, when he accepted the directorship of Columbia University's Teachers College Library. From 1931 to 1938, he was associate librarian of Yale University. He had a short stay, from 1938 to 1941, as librarian of the Cleveland Public Library. His final move was in 1941, when Rush became director of the University of North Carolina Library until he retired in 1954, ending a library career of nearly fifty years.

Rush was president of the Missouri Library Association (1912-1913), president of the Indiana Library Association (1918-1919), and vice-president of the American Library Association (1931-1932). He was among the first librarians to take an interest in microphotography, establishing a microphotographic laboratory at Yale. He was also influential as an advisor on library projects for the Carnegie Corporation.

ST. JOHN, FRANCIS REGIS (1908-1971) was born in Northampton, Massachusetts. He had his first taste of libraries as a teenager by working from 1919 to 1925 in the Forbes Library, the local public library in Northampton. While a student at Amherst College, he worked as an assistant in the library and completed his A.B. degree in 1931.

The next step for St. John was to take a job as stack supervisor in the New York Public Library and to graduate from Columbia's School of Library Service in 1932. In 1933-1934, he was promoted to desk supervisor of the main reading room at the New York Public Library, and from 1934 to 1939, he was a general assistant in both the preparations division and the director's office. In 1939, he became assistant director of the Enoch Pratt Free Library in Baltimore, under Joseph L. Wheeler.

In 1941, St. John returned to New York as chief of the New York Public Library's circulation department, responsible for the branch libraries. After the United States went to war, he was acting librarian and then assistant to the director of the U.S. Army Medical Library from 1943 to 1945. St. John resigned from the New York Public Library in 1947 to become director of library services for the U.S. Veterans Administration until he was appointed chief librarian of the Brooklyn Public Library in 1949, succeeding Milton J. Ferguson. His later professional activities included participating in the programs of the American and New York library associations, establishing a consulting firm that conducted a variety of surveys around the country, and finally serving as librarian from 1956 to 1971 of St. Anselm's College in Manchester, New Hampshire.

SAYERS, FRANCES CLARK (1897-1989) was long a leader in library service for children and in creating children's literature. She was of the tradition established earlier by Caroline Maria Hewins and Anne Carroll Moore. She was active as an anthologist, translator, and author of a number of works designed to stimulate children's reading.

Perhaps her most popular and influential writing is her long-famous "Lose Not the Nightingale," an essay "that was to librarians an irresistible voice directing them . . . to the best in all ramifications of library work with the young."

SCHENK, RACHEL KATHERINE (1899-1973) was the daughter of Swiss immigrants to New Philadelphia, Ohio. She graduated from Kent State Normal School in 1918 and was librarian of the Girard (Ohio) Free Library from 1925 to 1927. She received a diploma from the New York School of Librarians at Chautauqua in 1926. After joining the Purdue University staff, she earned a bachelor's degree in 1932, followed by a B.S. in library science from the Columbia School of Library Service and a master's degree from the University of Chicago Library School in 1945. She joined the faculty of the University of Wisconsin Library School and in 1951 became director of the school until 1963. From 1965 to 1969, she was on the faculty of the School of Library and Informational Science at the University of Wisconsin-Milwaukee, retiring in 1969. In recognition of services to the profession, the Wisconsin Library Association presented her with its first Citation of Merit.

SCHOMBURG, ARTHUR ALFONZO (1874-1938) was born in San Juan, Puerto Rico, the son of a black laundress and a German merchant. He was destined to become the leading collector and interpreter of materials relating to black history. Though not a librarian himself, he had a long association with the New York Public Library. He systematically collected books, manuscripts, letters, paintings, and anything else that dealt with the history and culture of his race. In 1926, the Carnegie Corporation purchased his collection and named it the Schomburg Collection of the Negro Division of History and Literature at the 135th Street Branch of the New York Public Library. After his retirement, Schomburg served as curator of the Negro collection at Fisk University, but in 1931, he returned to become curator of his own collection at the New York Public Library until his death in 1938.

SCHWAB, JOHN CHRISTOPHER (1865-1916) was born in New York City. He graduated from Yale University in 1886 and received a Ph.D. degree from Göttingen in 1889. Because he displayed both executive ability and scholarship, he was appointed librarian of Yale University in 1905. During his eleven-year tenure in that position, the library's collections increased substantially. Liberal policies were also adopted: longer hours for remaining open were established, the stacks were opened to qualified students, and more efficient methods were adopted for the purchase of books.

SCOGGIN, MARGARET CLARA (1905-1968) was born in Caruthersville, Missouri, and graduated from Radcliffe College in 1926. She spent a year at the University of London's School of Librarianship and later studied for a master's degree at Columbia's School of Library Service. She was a branch librarian for the New

York Public Library in the 1920s and 1930s. In 1945, she became host for a weekly book reviewing program on radio, a program that continued for fifteen years under the auspices of the station and for another seven years under the sponsorship of the New York Public Library. In 1952, she became the library's superintendent of work with young people and continued in that position until shortly before her death. She won numerous awards for her contributions to children's literature.

SEARS, MINNIE EARL (1873-1933) was born in Lafayette, Indiana. She received two degrees from Purdue University, in 1891 and 1893, and graduated from the University of Illinois Library School in 1900. From 1903 to 1907, she was head cataloger at the Bryn Mawr College Library, and from 1909 to 1914, she was head cataloger at the University of Minnesota Library. In 1914, she became the first assistant at the New York Public Library's reference-catalog division, remaining there until 1920. Her final move was in 1923, when she joined the H. W. Wilson Company. From 1927 to 1931, she taught in Columbia's School of Library Service.

Miss Sears produced a number of important reference works and bibliographic compilations. She is best remembered for her *List of Subject Headings for Small Libraries* (1923), which has gone through numerous editions and is widely used as a textbook. She edited the *Children's Catalog* (1925 and 1930), the *Song Index* (1926), *Essay and General Literature Index* (1931-1933), and ALA's *Standard Catalog for Public Libraries* (1927-1933).

SHARP, KATHARINE LUCINDA (1865-1914) was a disciple of Melvil Dewey and a pioneer in library education. She established the fourth library school in the country — the first in the Midwest — at Armour Institute in Chicago. After four years, the school was transferred to the University of Illinois at Urbana. Miss Sharp remained as director until 1907. She was a graduate of Northwestern University and of the New York State Library School at Albany.

Under Miss Sharp's direction, the entrance requirements at Illinois were raised, eventually to specify college graduation and two years of professional library courses for a bachelor of library science degree.

Miss Sharp made significant contributions to library school curriculum construction, with emphasis on practical applications rather than on the previously dominant theoretical approach. Textbooks on library science were later creations. During Miss Sharp's years as director, the Illinois school produced many of the library professional leaders.

SHAW, CHARLES BUNSEN (1894-1962) was born in Toledo, Ohio. He graduated from Clark University in 1914 and from the New York State Library School in 1920. He was librarian at the Woman's College of the University of North Carolina at Greensboro from 1920 to 1927. In 1927, he was appointed librarian of Swarthmore College and remained in that position until his death in 1962. He taught for summer sessions of the Columbia and Michigan library schools from 1930 to 1961 and at the Drexel University Library School during the spring semesters.

Shaw is best remembered for his *A List of Books for College Libraries* (ALA, 1931 and a supplement, 1940), prepared with the assistance of 200 librarians, professors, and other scholars.

SHAW, RALPH ROBERT (1907-1972) was born in Detroit, Michigan, but shortly thereafter moved to Cleveland, where he was employed as a page at the Cleveland Public Library. He held degrees from Western Reserve University and the Columbia Library School. For seven years, he served as a senior assistant and chief bibliographer of the Engineering Society's Library. In 1936, he was appointed director of the Gary (Indiana) Public Library and became a doctoral candidate at the University of Chicago Graduate Library School, from which he received a Ph.D. degree in 1950. In 1940, Shaw became director of the U.S. National

Agricultural Library, a position that he held until 1954. During that time, he made the USDA library one of the major governmental libraries and established his own reputation as a leading library administrator.

Shaw switched fields in 1954 by becoming a library educator, joining the Rutgers University Library School faculty and serving as dean from 1959 to 1961. He left Rutgers in 1964 to become assistant to the president, dean of libraries, and professor of library science at the University of Hawaii until 1969, when he retired. As a surveyor, he conducted major studies of several large public libraries in the United States and Canada and in Latin American, Indian, Pakistani, and Philippine libraries.

Other highlights in Shaw's career included presidency of the Indiana Library Association (1938-1939), presidency of the New Jersey Library Association (1962-1963), and presidency of the American Library Association (1956-1957). He was also instrumental in establishing the Scarecrow Press at Metuchen, New Jersey, in 1960 for publication of scholarly works of limited circulation. He filled a gap in U.S. national bibliography by publishing *American Bibliography: A Preliminary Checklist, 1801-1819*.

Shaw had an acerbic pen and tongue and not infrequently engaged in controversy with dissenters from his opinions. In general, however, he was a highly useful and constructive influence on the library profession.

SHAW, WILLIAM SMITH (1778-1826) was born in Haverhill, Massachusetts, and graduated from Harvard in 1798. For two years, he served as President John Adams's private secretary. From 1801 to 1804, he studied law in Boston and became a member of the bar. His aunt, Abigail Adams, stimulated his love for books. When the Boston Athenaeum was founded in 1807, Shaw became the librarian and remained in that position until 1822. He was intensely loyal to the athenaeum and was energetic in expanding its resources.

SHERA, JESSE HAUK (1903-1982) was a leading library educator and authority on documentation, classification, and the history of American libraries. He was born in Oxford, Ohio, and graduated from Miami University in Oxford in 1925. He received a master's degree in English from Yale in 1927 and a Ph.D. in library science from the University of Chicago in 1944. He began his library career as an assistant at the Miami University Library in Oxford. He went to Washington in 1940 to accept a position at the Library of Congress as chief of the census library project, and the next year he transferred to the Office of Strategic Services as deputy chief of the central information division of the research and analysis branch. From 1944 to 1952, he was at the University of Chicago, first as associate director of libraries and then as a member of the Graduate Library School faculty. In 1952, he became dean of Western Reserve University's School of Library Science. Starting in 1960, he also served as director of the school's center for documentation and communications research.

Shera was president of the Association of American Library Schools in 1964-1965. Earlier, from 1963 to 1964, he was president of the Ohio Library Association. He was a prolific author of books, journal articles, and reviews, including his well-known historical work *Foundations of the Public Library* (1949) and *Historians, Books and Libraries* (1953).

SHERMAN, CLARENCE EDGAR (1887-1974) was born in Brooklyn, New York. He graduated from Trinity College in Hartford and from the New York State Library School at Albany. From 1912 to 1917, he was assistant librarian of Amherst College Library, and from 1917 to 1922, he was with the Lyon (Massachusetts) Public Library. He served as assistant librarian from 1922 to 1930 at the Providence (Rhode Island) Public Library and was librarian at Providence from 1930 until his retirement in 1957. Achievements during that period included construction of a new library building, development of a modern system of branch libraries, establishment of a business branch, creation of a comprehensive stack storage plan for little-used materials, and an improvement in standards. Sherman was one of the founders of the New England Library Association. Honorary degrees were granted him by Trinity College, Brown University, and the University of Rhode Island.

SHOEMAKER, RICHARD HESTON (1907-1970) was born in Philadelphia and graduated from the University of Pennsylvania and the School of Library Service at Columbia. His early positions were with Temple University, the Mercantile Library of Philadelphia, and Washington and Lee University. He became librarian of the Newark Colleges of Rutgers University in 1947 and ten years later joined the faculty of the Rutgers Library School at the invitation of the dean, Ralph Shaw.

Shoemaker's major contribution to librarianship was as a bibliographer. He compiled *American Bibliography, A Preliminary Checklist, 1801-1819* and continued with *Checklist of American Imprints, 1820-1829.*

SHORES, LOUIS (1904-1981) was a native of Buffalo, New York. He graduated from the University of Toledo in 1926 and from the Columbia School of Library Service in 1928. He received a Ph.D. degree from George Peabody College in 1934. He began his library career as an assistant at the Toledo Public Library from 1918 to 1922. He was an assistant at the University of Toledo Library (1924-1926), a reference assistant at the New York Public Library (1926-1928), librarian of Fisk University (1928-1933), librarian of Peabody College (1933-1935), and director of the Peabody Library School (1933-1946). From 1942 to 1946, he was in military service in the United States and in the Far East. In 1946, he became dean of the Florida State University Library School in Tallahassee until 1967.

Shores was president of the Southeastern Library Association in 1950-1952 and president of the Florida Library Association in 1951-1952. He was awarded the Isabella Gilbert Mudge Citation in 1967 and was author of *Basic Reference Books* (1937 and 1939) and other works. From 1946 to 1960, he was associate editor of *Collier's Encyclopedia*, and from 1960 to 1981 he served as editor-in-chief.

Sibley, John Langdon (1804-1885) was born in Union, Maine, and graduated from Harvard in 1825. He was assistant librarian at Harvard for two periods, in 1825 and after 1841, and he held the latter position for fifteen yers. Following his second term, he was appointed librarian, succeeding Thaddeus William Harris. By the time that he retired in 1877, the book collection and endowed funds had grown substantially. In 1861, he began a card catalog of the library, an innovation at the time.

Failing eyesight forced Sibley to resign as librarian. His later years were devoted to literary and historical writings.

Smith, Carleton Sprague (1905-   ), a native of New York City, graduated with two degrees from Harvard, in 1927 and 1928. He received a Ph.D. degree from the University of Vienna in 1930. For twenty-eight years, from 1931 to 1959, he was chief of the New York Public Library's music division. At the same time, he taught history at Columbia University (1931-1933) and was on the music faculty of New York University after 1939.

Smith had a particular interest in promoting international exchange in music. He was an official delegate at the International Music Education Conference in Prague, Czechoslovakia, in 1936. The U.S. State Department sponsored his goodwill tour of South America in 1940. From 1944 to 1946, Smith served as cultural attaché at São Paulo, Brazil. After resigning his position with the New York Public Library in 1959, Smith was appointed director of New York University's Brazilian Institute.

Smith was president of the Music Library Association from 1936 to 1938 and president of the American Musicology Association from 1939 to 1940.

SMITH, CHARLES WESLEY (1877-1956) was born in Elizabeth City, North Carolina. He graduated from the University of Illinois in 1903 and received a B.L.S. degree in 1905 from the Illinois Library School. He became assistant librarian at the University of Washington immediately thereafter and advanced to the position of head librarian in 1929, remaining in that post until his retirement in 1947. He was also a member of the faculty of the University of Washington School of Library Science from 1913 to 1947. His entire career of forty-two years was spent in Seattle at the University of Washington.

Smith took a special interest in the development of a major collection on the history of the Pacific Northwest. He was a leader in founding the Pacific Northwest Library Association in 1909 and was its president from 1919 to 1920. He also initiated the establishment of the Pacific Northwest Bibliographic Center to reduce expensive competition among libraries in the Northwest.

SMITH, LLOYD PEARSALL (1822-1886) was a native of Philadelphia and a graduate of Haverford College. He became assistant librarian in 1849 of the Library Company of Philadelphia, of which his father was librarian. Smith remained identified with this library, founded by Benjamin Franklin, for the remainder of his life. Smith was the first editor of *Lippincott's Magazine* (1868-1869) and one of the original associate editors of the *Library Journal*, founded in 1876. Smith and his family were personal friends of Walt Whitman.

SMITH, MARY ALLEGRA (1869-1958) was born in Janesville, Wisconsin, and graduated from the University of Wisconsin in 1890. She was appointed librarian of Rhinelander from 1902 to 1905, librarian of Eau Claire from 1905 to 1910, and librarian of Madison for twenty-five years, starting in 1910. She added branches and expanded library service to hospitals and schools. She was president of the Wisconsin Library Association in 1913.

Her brother, Walter M. Smith, was librarian of the University of Wisconsin for many years.

SONNECK, OSCAR GEORGE THEODORE (1873-1928) was born in Jersey City, New Jersey, and grew up in Frankfurt-am-Main, Germany. After his education and travel in Europe, he returned to the United States in 1899. In 1902, he became the first chief of the Library of Congress' music division. He worked assiduously to develop this division into the largest and most comprehensive collection of music and books on music in the country and one of the leading music libraries of the world.

In 1917, Sonneck resigned from the Library of Congress to join the G. Schirmer Company, a music publisher in New York. He held a managerial position there until his death in 1928.

SPAIN, FRANCES LANDER (1903-   ) was born in Jacksonville, Florida. She graduated from Winthrop College in 1925 and from the Emory University Library School in 1936. She holds master's and doctoral degrees from the University of Chicago Graduate Library School. She began her professional career as an assistant in the children's department of the Jacksonville (Florida) Public Library from 1919 to 1921. She served as librarian of the Winthrop Training School from 1936 to 1945, as librarian of Winthrop College from 1945 to 1949, and as assistant director of the School of Library Science at the University of Southern California in Los Angeles from 1949 to 1953. She spent a year in Thailand, 1951-1952, developing a program of library training in Bangkok under a Fulbright grant. In 1953, Mrs. Spain became coordinator of children's services at the New York Public Library.

Mrs. Spain has been active in a number of professional organizations: she was president of the South Carolina Library Association in 1947, president of the library education division of the ALA from 1959 to 1960, and president of the American Library Association from 1960 to 1961. She has been a visiting lecturer at Columbia, Pratt Institute, Rutgers, and Syracuse library schools.

SPOFFORD, AINSWORTH RAND (1825-1908) was born in Gilmanton, New Hampshire. He entered librarianship through an appointment in 1861 as chief assistant to John G. Stephenson, librarian of Congress. Following Stephenson's resignation in 1864, Spofford was appointed librarian of Congress by President Abraham Lincoln in 1864, the last year of the Civil War, and Stephenson dedicated the next forty-three years to making the institution a truly national library. Spofford has been termed "the first giant" to occupy the position of librarian of Congress. In 1870, a revised copyright law was passed requiring books, magazines, music, photographs, prints, and maps to be deposited in the library. Materials that had previously gone to the Departments of State and Interior and to the Smithsonian Institution were also turned over to the library.

Other major developments under Spofford's direction were purchase of the great Peter Force collection of Americana, construction of a new library building (starting in 1886 with occupancy in 1897), and publication of a two-volume catalog of the Library of Congress — *Index of Subjects* — listing all of the books in the library. By 1897, the library's holdings had assumed major proportions.

After the removal of the library from its old quarters in the Capitol to its own building in 1897, Spofford gave up the top position to John Russell Young and served as chief assistant from 1897 until his death in 1908. Under Spofford's administration, the Library of Congress grew from about 600,000 volumes in 1861 to more than one million in 1897, laying the foundation for a great national library.

STEARNS, LUTIE EUGENIA (1866-1943) was a founding member of the Wisconsin Library Association and helped to establish the Wisconsin Free Library Commission in 1895. In 1903, she helped to set up the commission's traveling library department to take books to isolated areas and farmers. Over a period of seventeen years, she helped to establish 150 free libraries and 1,480 traveling libraries in Wisconsin.

She was a library field worker of extraordinary devotion and effectiveness. She was responsible for establishing traveling libraries in Wisconsin and for advancing library work with children. She was head of the circulation department at the Milwaukee Public Library from 1890 to 1897, a member of the Wisconsin Free Library Commission from 1897 to 1914, a lecturer on libraries in library schools throughout the country, and author of *Essentials in Library Administration* (1922).

STEIG, LEWIS FRANCIS (1909-1990) was born in North Tonawanda, New York, and graduated from the University of Buffalo in 1931. He completed master's degrees at Harvard (1932) and at the University of Michigan (1933). He held two professional degrees from the University of Chicago, including a Ph.D. in 1936. He was librarian of Stetson University (1935-1936), librarian of Hamilton College (1936-1943), associate director of the University of Illinois Library School (1943-1947), and director of the University of Southern California Library School (1947-1955). He was also university librarian from 1948 to 1971. Steig was a Fulbright lecturer at the University of the Philippines in 1954-1955 and taught at the University of Ankara Library Institute in 1957-1959. He was president of the ALA library education division in 1946-1947.

Steig's final professional appointment was at Northern Illinois University, where he was department chairman in library science from 1971 to 1978. He retired in 1979.

STEINER, BERNARD CHRISTIAN (1867-1926) was born in Guilford, Connecticut. He graduated from Yale in 1888 and received a Ph.D. degree from Johns Hopkins University in 1891. In 1892, he was elected to the librarianship of the Enoch Pratt Free Library in Baltimore, to succeed his father. The number of branches of the library under his direction increased from six to twenty-five and reached every neighborhood. He held the position for thirty-four years until his death in 1926.

STEINER, LEWIS HENRY (1827-1892), the father of Bernard Christian Steiner, was born in Frederick, Maryland. He graduated from Marshall College in Mercersburg, Pennsylvania, and received a degree in medicine from the University of Pennsylvania. When Enoch Pratt built and endowed the library in Baltimore named for him, he brought Lewis Steiner from Frederick to be its librarian. The library was opened to the public in 1886, and from that time until his sudden death in 1892, Steiner served as its head. He was president of the American Academy of Medicine in 1878.

STEPHENSON, JOHN G. (1828-1883), another short-term occupant of the position of librarian of Congress, was appointed by President Lincoln in 1861 to replace Meehan. In 1864, Stephenson was forced to resign because of "speculations created by war," specifically, a controversy involving an English bookseller.

STEVENSON, BURTON EGBERT (1872-1962) was born in Chillicothe, Ohio, and attended Princeton University from 1890 to 1893. He accepted the position as librarian of the Chillicothe Public Library in 1897 and remained on the job intermittently until his retirement in 1957, fifty-eight years later. With the coming of World War I, Stevenson was appointed to direct the Army War Service in Paris. More than three million books and magazines were distributed to American troops. This program led to the establishment of the American Library in Paris in 1920; Stevenson served as director of this library for five years.

Stevenson is best known in the library world for his anthologies: *The Home Book of Verse, The Home Book of Proverbs, The Home Book of Bible Quotations*, and others. He was also a prolific novelist.

STROHM, ADAM JULIUS (1870-1951) was born in Sweden and graduated from college there in 1888. He came to the United States in 1892 and in 1906 received a B.L.S. degree from the University of Illinois Library School. For the next decade, he held several positions, but he was chosen for a major opening in 1911 when he became librarian of the Detroit Public Library, serving thirty years until his retirement in 1941. Strohm was admired as a strong professional leader. In 1918-1919, he was elected president of the Michigan Library Association, and in 1930-1931, he served as president of the American Library Association.

STUMMVOLL, JOSEF LEOPOLD (1902-1982) was born in Baden, Austria. He received a master's degree and a doctorate in science from Vienna Technical University. He worked in Germany as research librarian and deputy director of the Berlin Patent Office Library and as research librarian and director of the reading department at the Deutsche Bücherei in Leipzig from 1927 to 1937.

In 1946, Stummvoll was appointed deputy librarian of the Austrian National Library and in 1949 was given the title of general director. Under his guidance, the library underwent extensive reorganization. The library holds one of the world's major collections of incunabula, papyri, and manuscripts. It collects all material published in or about Austria or written by Austrians abroad. The library publishes the official Austrian national bibliography.

Stummvoll was advisor to the Turkish government in the building and organization of the Library of the College of Agriculture and Veterinary Medicine in Ankara in 1933 and was appointed by UNESCO in 1952 as chief advisor for the development of Iranian libraries.

In 1959, Stummvoll was appointed to a four-year term as United Nations librarian. One of his first duties was to plan a new building for the library financed by a Ford Foundation grant.

Back in Vienna, Stummvoll resumed direction of the Austrian National Library. Budgets, staff, and holdings more than doubled during his administration, restoring the library to its former rank as one of Europe's most important cultural centers.

SWANK, RAYNARD COE (1912-   ) was born in Butler, Ohio, and graduated from the College of Wooster in 1934. He holds a B.S. in library science from Western Reserve University (1937) and a doctorate from the University of Chicago Graduate Library School (1944). He held various types of positions at the libraries of the University of Colorado, the University of Chicago, and the University of Minnesota, from 1937 to 1946. From 1946 to 1948, he was librarian of the University of Oregon, and from 1948 to 1962, he was director of the Stanford University libraries. In 1962, he became dean of the School of Librarianship at the University of California at Berkeley. From 1959 to 1961, Swank was director of the ALA International Relations Office.

Swank has been involved in extensive foreign travel. In 1961, he was a member of an American delegation to the Soviet Union, and from 1963 to 1964, he was a consultant for the Ford Foundation in Southeast Asia. In 1964, he served as a consultant to the Chinese University at Hong Kong. He has participated in a number of influential library surveys, including that of Stanford University with Louis R. Wilson in 1947 and that of the Midwest Inter-Library Center with Stephen McCarthy in 1964.

TAUBER, MAURICE F. (1908-1980), born in Norfolk, Virginia, was amazingly versatile. He established a reputation as an expert in the field of technical services, was a joint author with Louis R. Wilson of a standard work, *The University Library*, was editor of *College & Research Libraries*, served as a veteran library surveyor, and was a longtime faculty member of Columbia's School of Library Service. He held degrees from Temple University, from Columbia, and from Chicago's Graduate Library School.

He began his library experience as a student assistant and supervisor at the night desk at Temple, then became head of the Temple Library's cataloging department. At Chicago, he was much influenced by several members of the faculty — Wilson, Joeckel, and Waples, in particular. After completing his doctoral dissertation, dealing with reclassification and recataloging, Tauber was appointed to the University of Chicago Library staff and as an assistant professor in the Graduate Library School.

The Tauber surveys related to numerous institutions: Columbia, Cornell, South Carolina, Dartmouth, Barnard, Jewish Theological Seminary of America, Bowdoin College, and others. As a Fulbright scholar in 1962, Tauber surveyed several hundred libraries in Australia. Throughout his career, he was an outspoken advocate of the Library of Congress classification.

Other high points in Tauber's career were his appointment as Melvil Dewey Professor of Library Science at Columbia in 1954, his active interest in the planning and design of library buildings, his authorship of a biography of Louis R. Wilson, and his participation in numerous library organizations over a period of forty years. He also served as president of the ALA division of cataloging and classification.

THOMPSON, LAWRENCE SIDNEY (1916-1986) was born in Raleigh, North Carolina. He graduated with an A.B. degree in 1934 and a Ph.D. degree in 1938 from the University of North Carolina. He received a master's degree in 1935 from the University of Chicago in Latin and Germanic languages and an A.B. in library science from the University of Michigan in 1940. He was a student of Germanic languages at Upsala University in 1938 and at Lund University in 1939. His professional positions included assistant to the librarian of Iowa State College (1940-1942), special agent of the FBI, U.S. Department of Justice (1942-1945), bibliographer with the U.S. Department of Agriculture Library (1945-1946), librarian of Western Michigan College (1946-1948), and librarian of the University of Kentucky (1948-1966).

Thompson was an advisor to the Turkish Ministry of Education in Ankara from 1951 to 1952. His considerable writings related mainly to classical and romance languages.

THWAITES, REUBEN GOLD (1853-1913) was born in Dorchester, Massachusetts. He became superintendent-secretary of the Wisconsin State Historical Society in 1887, succeeding Lyman C. Draper, and held that position for the next twenty-six years.

As secretary of the Wisconsin Historical Society, he expanded the serviceability of the institution by building up its manuscript collection and making the collection available to scholars at the University of Wisconsin. His *Jesuit Relations and Allied Documents* (seventy-three volumes, 1896-1901), with its fine annotations and translations, established his reputation as one of the best historical editors of his day. He was managing editor of the *Wisconsin State Journal* from 1876 to 1886, superintendent-secretary of the State Historical Society of Wisconsin from 1887 to 1913, president of the American Library Association in 1899-1900, vice-chairman of the Wisconsin Free Library Commission, and an active member of the American Historical Society.

TISSERANT, EUGENE CARDINAL (1884-1972) was born in Nancy, France, and graduated from the College of St. Sigisbert in Nancy in 1900. He became a student assistant at the library of Major Seminary of Nancy and began the study of Ethiopic, Syrian, Arabic, Hebrew, and Assyrian languages, all of which were important for his primary interest — the study of the Old Testament. In 1907, he became curator of Oriental manuscripts in the Vatican Library. After active service in the French army in World War I, Tisserant returned to the Vatican Library in 1919. There he performed a variety of duties, supervising the modernization of the library and the construction of a new wing to the library building in 1927. He traveled widely in the United States and elsewhere, visiting libraries and attending library conferences. Officially, Tisserant was librarian and archivist of the Roman Catholic

Church and dean of the College of Cardinals. He was named a cardinal by Pope Pius XI in 1936.

TITCOMB, MARY L. (1857-1931), a native of Farmington, New Hampshire, pioneered several important library undertakings. She was librarian of the Washington County (Maryland) Free Library, the first chartered county library in the United States. The base for the library, opened in 1901, was Hagerstown. Within five years, sixty-six deposit stations had been set up outside Hagerstown. To reach people in isolated areas, a book wagon was planned, and by 1904 it had become a reality. The first books were carried in a hired, horse-drawn covered wagon driven by the library janitor. Shortly thereafter, the library procured its own wagon, drawn by two mules. By 1916, an automobile was being used. The library's financial problems were eased by a grant of $25,000 from the Carnegie Corporation for books and equipment. Another innovation started by Miss Titcomb was the Washington County Free Library training class. From 1924 to 1931, this class provided a curriculum that paralleled that of professional library schools, and it produced useful assistants, some of whom later became professional librarians.

TREZZA, ALPHONSE F. (1920-   ) was born in Philadelphia and graduated from the University of Pennsylvania in 1948. He holds a B.S. degree from Drexel and an M.S. from the University of Pennsylvania. He was in military service in South Korea from 1946 to 1947. He has held positions with the following institutions: the New York Academy of Medicine, Columbia University Libraries, Stevens Institute of Technology, Yale University Library, the University of Michigan Library, the University of California at San Diego, and the University of Pennsylvania. Trezza was executive secretary of the Catholic Library Association and editor of the *Catholic Library World* from 1956 to 1961. He was also associate executive secretary of the American Library Association and secretary of the library education division section of the ALA from 1960 to 1970. He was Illinois state librarian from 1970 to 1974. Since 1982, he has been on the faculty of the Florida State University Library School at Tallahassee.

TUTTLE, HELEN WELCH (1914-   ) was born in Laural, Kansas. She graduated from the University of Kansas in 1935 and received a master's degree in mathematics from Kansas in 1936. Her preparation for the library profession came with a degree from the University of Illinois Library School in 1942. Her library career of thirty-seven years has concentrated on technical services, especially acquisitions. For almost three decades, she was head of the University of Illinois Library Acquisitions Department, and she played a major role in the growth and development of that library's notable collections in many fields. She joined the Princeton University staff as assistant university librarian for technical services in 1968 and remained in that position until her retirement in 1979.

Mrs. Tuttle has served on a number of ALA committees. She has been president of the ALA resources and technical services division and was chairperson of the ALA committee on future ALA structure.

TYLER, ALICE SARAH (1859-1944), was born in Illinois and received her professional training in librarianship at Armour Institute (after 1893, the University of Illinois Library School). From 1887 to 1893, she was an assistant in the Decatur (Illinois) Public Library. She then transferred to the position of catalog librarian at the Cleveland Public Library from 1895 to 1900. In 1900, she became secretary of the newly organized Iowa State Library Commission until 1913. Ten new libraries were established while she was secretary. Library extension work was actively promoted, and she directed a summer library school concurrently with her duties as secretary.

Miss Tyler's high standing in the library profession was recognized by her election to various offices: she was president of the

League of Library Commissions in 1906, a member of the American Library Institute (one of a hundred chosen by the American Library Association), president of the Ohio Library Association in 1916-1917, president of the Association of American Library Schools in 1918-1919, and president of the American Library Association in 1920-1921.

In 1913, Miss Tyler became director of the Western Reserve University Library School; in 1925, she was promoted to become dean of the school. Miss Tyler was administrative head of the Western Reserve school for sixteen years, during which it became fully accredited by the ALA board of education.

ULVELING, RALPH A. (1902-1980) was born in Adrian, Minnesota. He graduated from DePaul University in 1922 and won a B.S. in library science from Columbia in 1928. His library career began at the Newberry Library in Chicago from 1924 to 1926 and continued at the Amarillo (Texas) Public Library, where he served as librarian from 1926 to 1927. In 1928, he was appointed chief of branches at the Detroit Public Library. He was promoted to the associate directorship in 1934, and in 1941, he became director of the Detroit Public Library, a post that he held for twenty-six years. Under his direction, eleven new branches were added, and the municipal reference library, the rare book room, and the automotive history department were organized. The main library was divided into subject departments, and in 1963, a major addition to the main library building was opened.

Ulveling was recognized as a dynamic leader in the library profession. He was president of the Michigan Library Association from 1937 to 1938, during which time the state achieved the first state aid program. He had a particular interest in adult education and from 1935 to 1940 was an active member of the ALA adult education board and of the American Association for Adult Education. He served as president of the American Library Association in 1945-1946. With his longtime associate Charles M. Mohrhardt, who later became director of the Detroit Public Library, Ulveling was a building consultant for thirty public libraries and one state library. In 1946, he received the ALA Lippincott Award. He was married to Elizabeth Baer, a distinguished children's librarian at Detroit.

UTLEY, GEORGE BURWELL (1876-1946) was born in Hartford, Connecticut, and graduated from Brown University in 1899. He was offered and accepted the position of assistant librarian of the Watkinson Library in Hartford. In 1901, he moved to Baltimore to head the Maryland Diocesan Library of the Episcopal Church, where he stayed for four years. From 1905 to 1910, Utley was librarian of the Jacksonville (Florida) Public Library. The next important shift was his appointment in 1910 to become secretary of the American Library Association, succeeding Charles Hadley. Utley remained with the ALA for nine years, spending part of the time in Washington (1917-1919) as executive secretary of the ALA library war service committee. Another opportunity came to him in 1920, when he became director of the Newberry Library, a position that he held until 1942. During those twenty-two years, the resources of the Newberry Library grew extensively in American history, in English and American literature, in music, and in genealogy — thus establishing future collection policies.

Utley was elected president of the American Library Association for the 1922-1923 term. He was president of the Illinois Library Association in 1924-1925 and president of the American Library Institute from 1937 to 1939. His last major publication was *The Librarian's Conference of 1853.*

VAIL, ROBERT WILLIAM GLENROIE (1890-1966) was born in Victor, New York. He graduated from Cornell University and in 1915-1916 attended the New York Public Library School. He began his professional career as librarian of the Minnesota Historical Society. This was followed by a position with the Roosevelt Memorial Association and a return to the New York Public Library to head the American history division. Vail served as joint editor of the final sections of Sabin's *Dictionary of Books Relating to America*, a work completed in 1936.

Vail became librarian of the American Antiquarian Society in Worcester, Massachusetts, and remained there until 1940. He left that position to become librarian of the New York State Library in Albany, where he remained for four years, 1940-1944.

VAN HOESEN, HENRY BARTLETT (1885-1965) was born in Truxton, New York, and graduated from Hobart College in 1905. He received an A.M. in 1906 and a Ph.D. in 1912 from Princeton University. He had extended stays abroad — at the American School of Classical Studies in Rome from 1907 to 1908 and at the University of Munich in Germany from 1908 to 1909. From 1909 to 1911, he was an instructor in classics at Princeton, and from 1912 to 1915, he taught at Western Reserve University.

Van Hoesen entered the library profession by becoming curator of manuscripts and rare books at Princeton from 1915 to 1916. Still at Princeton, he was appointed assistant librarian and held that position from 1916 to 1929. He then moved to Brown University as an associate librarian from 1929 to 1930 and as librarian from 1930 to 1949. After 1930, he was also named John Hay Professor of Bibliography. From 1934 to 1936, he was president of the American Library Institute.

Van Hoesen's published works related mainly to paleography and papyrology. A standard work in its field is his *Bibliography, Practical, Enumerative and Historical* (1928), coauthored with Frank K. Walter.

Van Name, Addison (1835-1922) was born in Chenango, New York, and graduated from Yale in 1858. He was responsible for making the Yale collection of Oriental literature one of the best in the United States. He was librarian of the American Oriental Society from 1873 to 1905 and of the Connecticut Academy of Arts and Sciences from 1865 to 1905. His chief work, however, was as librarian of Yale for forty years, overseeing the growth of its collections from about 44,500 volumes to 300,000. He became librarian emeritus in 1905.

Van Patten, Nathan (1887-1956) was born in Niskayuna, New York, and was educated at the Union Classical Institute. He spent his early years, from 1907 to 1917, as a public school teacher and bookseller. His introduction to librarianship came when he served as librarian of the Wolcott Gibbs Library at the College of the City of New York from 1917 to 1920, from which he proceeded to become reference librarian, from 1920 to 1921, of the Massachusetts Institute of Technology. He was chief librarian of Queen's University in Kingston, Ontario, Canada, from 1923 to 1927 and then director of Stanford University libraries from 1927 to 1947. From 1947 to 1952, he was a professor of bibliography at Stanford. He also advised Yale University, the Hoover Library at Stanford, and the Library of Congress on the development of collections in special fields. His published writings concerned technological subjects, chemistry and medicine, music, and the history of printing.

Vinton, Frederic (1817-1890) was born in Boston and graduated from Amherst College in 1837. His first library experience was to catalog the large private library of his brother, Alfred

Vinton. In 1856, he was appointed assistant librarian of the Boston Public Library under its first librarian, Edward Capen. He helped to prepare the library's printed catalogs and to classify its collections. In 1865, he became first assistant of the Library of Congress, under Ainsworth Rand Spofford, where he was again occupied with preparing catalogs from 1867 to 1872.

In 1873, Vinton became the first full-time librarian of the College of New Jersey, now Princeton University. Under his direction, the library's collections grew from 18,000 volumes to 70,000 volumes by the time of his death in 1890. He also prepared and published a scholarly and useful subject catalog of the library in 1884.

Vinton was one of the founders of the American Library Association.

VON OESEN, ELAINE (1913-   ) was born in Wilmington, North Carolina, and graduated from Lenoir Rhyne College in 1938. She earned a B.A. in library science in 1940 and an M.A. in history in 1951 from the University of North Carolina. She was a county librarian in North Carolina and Georgia (1940-1943), an army librarian (1943-1944), a faculty member of the School of Library Science at the University of North Carolina (1947-1952), and a library extension service worker for North Carolina State Library (1952-1965). She was appointed assistant state librarian at North Carolina State Library (1965-1975). von Oesen was president of the Southeastern Library Association from 1968 to 1970 and editor of *North Carolina Libraries* from 1953 to 1957. The North Carolina Library Association awarded her life membership in 1976. Her great contribution to librarianship was her understanding and sharing of library law.

VOSPER, ROBERT (1913-   ) has had an exceptional professional career, including the position as administrator of the libraries at the University of Kansas, the University of California at Los Angeles, and the Clark Library. He was president of the American

Library Association in 1965-1967. He also held a professorship at the UCLA Graduate School of Library and Information Science from 1961 to 1973. Vosper is a native of Portland, Oregon, and holds degrees from the University of Oregon and the University of California Library School at Berkeley.

One of Vosper's prime interests has been international librarianship, and he has been prominent in the International Federation of Library Associations (IFLA) since 1960, serving as program chairman for the fiftieth anniversary celebration in Brussels in 1977, and as vice-president from 1971 to 1976. IFLA fellowships have been established for a three-year period, with funds provided by the Council on Library Resources, and are being named for Robert Vosper "in recognition of his long and effective commitment to the cause of international librarianship."

WAGMAN, FREDERICK HERBERT (1912-) was born in Springfield, Massachusetts, and graduated from Amherst College in 1933. He earned a master's degree from Columbia University in 1934 and a Ph.D. in 1942. After a year's study in Germany and Switzerland, he taught German at Columbia, Amherst, and the University of Minnesota, from 1933 to 1942. In 1945, Wagman joined the Library of Congress under Luther H. Evans. He served the Library of Congress in various capacities over an eight-year period, most prominently as director of the processing department, as deputy chief assistant librarian, and as director of administration. Publication of the Library of Congress catalog began while he was in charge of the processing department.

In 1953, Wagman left the Library of Congress to succeed Warner Rice as director of the University of Michigan Library at Ann Arbor, retiring in 1981. During his administration there, a new undergraduate library was opened in 1958, and a storage library and new medical school library were added.

Wagman was president of the Michigan Library Association in 1959-1960 and president of the American Library Association in 1963-1964.

WALTER, FRANK KELLER (1874-1945) was born in Mount Pleasant, Pennsylvania. He graduated from Haverford College in 1899 and received a B.L.S. degree from the New York State Library School in 1906. His first professional job was as a reference assistant at the Brooklyn Public Library. In 1907, he returned to the New York State Library School, first as assistant to the director and then, from 1908 to 1919, as vice-director. After brief periods of teaching in the Illinois and Michigan library schools, he was appointed, in 1921, librarian of the University of Minnesota. He remained there until his retirement in 1943. Under Walter's direction, the University of Minnesota Library was developed into one of the nation's important research libraries. Between 1921 and 1943, the book collection increased from one-quarter million to more than one and one-quarter million volumes. The library school, established in 1928, also flourished under his guidance.

In professional organizations, Walter was president of the New York Library Association (1915-1916), president of the Association of American Library Schools (1919-1920), and president of the Minnesota Library Association (1922-1923).

Walter was an active author. Of lasting importance is his *Bibliography, Practical, Enumerative, Historical* (1928), with Henry B. Van Hoesen as coauthor.

WARREN, ALTHEA HESTER (1886-1958) was born in Waukegan, Illinois, and graduated from the University of Chicago in 1908. She attended the Wisconsin University Library School in 1909. Her first professional position was as a branch librarian in a poverty-stricken neighborhood of Chicago. She served next in a branch where there were many foreign-born residents. In 1915, she moved to San Diego and spent ten years as librarian of the San Diego Public Library. She made a major move in 1926 when she became assistant librarian of the rapidly growing Los Angeles Public Library. A new central building was opened in 1926, and in 1933, Miss Warren assumed the position of head librarian. She remained there until her retirement in 1947. She was president of the California Library Association in 1921-1922 and in 1943-1944 was president of the American Library Association. Miss Warren directed the Victory Books Campaign, which collected five million books for World War II soldiers.

After giving up her position as chief librarian of the Los Angeles Public Library, Miss Warren engaged in library school teaching at the Universities of Michigan, Wisconsin, and Southern California.

WATTERSON, GEORGE (1783-1854) was born aboard a ship in New York Harbor. After a short stay in the legal profession, he was a newspaper editor in Washington. In 1815, he was appointed by President Madison to be the first full-time librarian of Congress. His first job was to receive and arrange Thomas Jefferson's library, which had just been purchased. Soon after his appointment in 1815, Watterson's *Catalogue of the Library of Congress* went to press, following Jefferson's scheme of classification. He antagonized President Andrew Jackson, who summarily dismissed him in March 1829. During his tenure, the collections of the Library of Congress grew substantially, the book budget was increased, and the library began to realize Watterson's vision of a national repository for American cultural history.

WEBER, DAVID CARTER (1924-   ) was born in Waterville, Maine, the son of the head of Colby College's English department. He graduated from Colby College in 1947 and from the Columbia School of Library Service in 1948. He received a master's degree in history from Harvard in 1953 and a master's degree in library science from Rutgers University in 1956. He began his library career as a cataloger at the Harvard College Library from 1948 to 1950. He became assistant to the director at Harvard College in 1950 and held that position until 1957, when he became assistant director and assistant librarian until 1961. He went on to Stanford University in 1961, first as assistant director of libraries (1961-1965), then as associate director (1965-1969), and since 1969 as director. He has served as a consultant for a number of academic libraries. He is coauthor with R. D. Rogers of a standard work, *University Library Administration* (1971). In 1981-1982, Weber was president of the Association of College and Research Libraries. During World War II, from 1943 to 1946, he served with the U.S. Army.

WEDGEWORTH, ROBERT (1937-   ) is a native of Ennis, Texas. He is a graduate of Wabash College and of the University of Illinois Library School. He has worked as a cataloger at the Kansas City Public Library (1961-1962), as assistant librarian at Park College (1962-1964), as librarian of Meramec Community College (1964-1966), and as assistant chief acquisitions librarian at Brown University (1966-1969). From 1971 to 1972, he served as a professor at Rutgers University, and he was executive director of the American Library Association from 1972 to 1985. In 1985, Wedgeworth was appointed dean of the Columbia University School of Library Service. He was editor-in-chief of the *ALA Yearbook* from 1976 to 1985 and of the *ALA World Encyclopedia of Library and Information Services* (1986 edition). He received an honorary doctorate from Park College in 1973.

WEST, THERESA ELMENDORF (1855-1932) was married to another well-known librarian, Henry Elmendorf. She was engaged in library service for nearly sixty years. From 1880 to 1892, she was deputy assistant librarian of the Milwaukee Public Library and in 1892 was promoted to city librarian, the first woman librarian of a large city. In that position, she promoted children's rooms and library service to all elements of the population.

Henry Elmendorf was librarian of the St. Joseph (Missouri) Public Library and later was appointed city librarian in Buffalo,

New York, a post that he held until his death in 1906. His successor as vice-librarian was Mrs. Elmendorf, who remained in that position until her retirement in 1926. In 1911-1912, she became ALA's first woman president. She was also president of the New York Library Association in 1903-1904.

WHEELER, JOSEPH LEWIS (1884-1970) was born in Dorchester, Massachusetts, and graduated from Brown University with Ph.D. and M.A. degrees (1906-1907). He received B.L.S. and M.L.S. degrees from the New York State Library School (1909-1925). He was an assistant at the Providence Public Library and at the Brown University Library (1902-1907), an assistant librarian at the Washington (D.C.) Public Library (1909-1911), a librarian at the Jacksonville (Florida) Public Library (1911-1912), an assistant librarian at the Los Angeles Public Library (1912-1915), a librarian at Youngstown, Ohio (1915-1926), and a librarian at the Enoch Pratt Library in Baltimore (1926-1945).

Wheeler was extremely active as a surveyor and consultant for more than 170 projects and was widely recognized as an expert on library buildings. He wrote extensively on library buildings. His *Practical Administration of Public Libraries* (1962), coauthored by Herbert Goldhor, is a standard work.

Wheeler was president of the Ohio Library Association in 1921. He received the ALA Lippincott Award in 1961 and was an honorary life member of the American Library Association.

WHITE, CARL MILTON (1903-1983) was born in Burnett, Oklahoma, and graduated from Oklahoma Baptist University in 1925. He received a doctorate in philosophy from Cornell University and a B.S. in library science from Columbia. He began his library career as librarian of Fisk University from 1934 to 1938. He was then librarian of the University of North Carolina (1938-1940) and director of the library and library school at the University of Illinois (1940-1943). In 1943, he became director of libraries at Columbia University and continued in that position until

1953. He also served as dean of the School of Library Service at Columbia University from 1943 to 1954. From 1943 to 1962, he was professor of library services at Columbia and then became a program specialist for the Ford Foundation.

His foreign service included the directorship of the Institute of Librarianship at the University of Ankara from 1959 to 1961 and serving as library advisor to the federal government of Nigeria from 1962 to 1964. White was editor of *College and Research Libraries* from 1941 to 1948.

WHITEHILL, WALTER MUIR (1905-1978) was born in Cambridge, Massachusetts. He graduated from Harvard in 1926 and received a Ph.D. degree from the University of London in 1934. He was assistant director of the Peabody Museum of Salem from 1936 to 1942 and director of the Boston Athenaeum from 1946 to 1973. He was the author of a number of historical works, concerned primarily with Boston institutions, and was on the editorial board for the publication of the Adams and Benjamin Franklin papers. Whitehill progressed from lieutenant to commander in the U.S. Naval Reserves from 1942 to 1946.

WHITNEY, JAMES LYMAN (1835-1910) was a native of Northampton, Massachusetts. He received two degrees from Yale, an A.B. in 1856 and an M.A. in 1865. After several years in publishing and bookselling, he became assistant librarian of the Cincinnati Public Library in 1868. In 1869, he joined the staff of the Boston Public Library, where he was destined to remain for the next forty years of his life. For twenty-five years, he was chief of the catalog department, and in 1899, he was appointed librarian of the Boston Public Library. He was forced to retire early because of poor health. He was the compiler and editor of a number of large bibliographical works.

Whitney was active in the affairs of the American Library Association and from 1882 to 1886 served as ALA treasurer.

WILLIAMSON, CHARLES CLARENCE (1877-1965) was born in Salem, Ohio. He graduated from Western Reserve University in 1904 and received a Ph.D. degree from Columbia University in 1907. He was chief of the New York Public Library's economics and sociology division (1911-1914), librarian of the New York City Municipal Reference Library (1914-1918), chief of the New York Public Library's economics division (1919-1921), and director of the Rockefeller's Information Service (1921-1926).

When the New York State Library School and the New York Public Library School merged at Columbia University in 1926, Williamson was appointed dean of the School of Library Service and director of libraries, a position in which he remained until his retirement in 1943. His appointment was doubtless influenced by a landmark work, *Training for Library Service* (1923), based on a survey sponsored by the Carnegie Corporation.

WILSON, HALSEY WILLIAM (1868-1954) was born in Wilmington, Vermont. Until 1889, he was employed at various jobs, mainly as a bookseller. Except for working on weekends at the Minneapolis Public Library in the early 1890s, Wilson lacked any practical experience as a librarian. Wilson noted, however, the need for an accurate, up-to-date record of currently published books. The first issue of the *Cumulative Book Index* appeared in February 1898. In 1899, Wilson published the *United States Catalog*. Not long after, in 1901, the *Readers' Guide to Periodical Literature* was launched. The *Book Review Digest* followed in 1905, as well as other reference works. Eventually, the H. W. Wilson Company became the world's foremost publisher of bibliographical and reference works. To assure financial security, the "service" basis was adopted for pricing — a sliding scale of fees based on the extent of holdings of subscribing libraries.

Wilson developed close relationships with the library profession by joining professional associations, promoting bibliographical projects, and sponsoring library awards.

WILSON, LOUIS ROUND (1876-1979) was nationally and internationally known as the dean of American university librarianship. He was the mentor for generations of men and women who rose to the top in the academic library world.

Wilson was born in the village of Lenoir in the Blue Ridge Mountain area of western North Carolina. He attended Haverford College for three years, leaving in 1898. He received four degrees from the University of North Carolina, including a Ph.D. in English in 1905 and an honorary doctorate in 1934. He served as librarian of the University of North Carolina from 1901 to 1932, a period during which he was also director of the Extension Bureau (1912-1921), director of the University of North Carolina Press (1922-1932), founder and director of the School of Library Science (1931-1932), editor of the *Alumni Review* (1912-1924), and chairman of the North Carolina Library Commission (1909-1916).

Wilson was also active in library associations: he was president of the North Carolina Library Association (1910, 1921-1923, and 1930-1931), president of the Southeastern Library Association (1924-1926), president of the American Library Association (1935-1936), and president of the Association of American Library Schools (1938-1939).

Wilson was a trailblazer in library surveys, developing methods that were emulated widely. Among the institutions covered by his studies were the Universities of Georgia, Florida, South Carolina, Columbia, Cornell, and Stanford. He wrote extensively in book, report, and periodical form. A standard text, *The University Library* (1945), was coauthored with Maurice Tauber.

Wilson's greatest impact on American librarianship in general was made as dean of the University of Chicago Graduate Library School, a position that he filled from 1932 to 1942. This period was generally regarded as the school's golden age, when it made educational history, had a distinguished faculty, produced many scholarly publications, developed a sound doctoral program, and placed its graduates in leading posts in college and university library administration.

It is likely that Wilson's first love was always the University of North Carolina. He was a key advisor there to every president for thirty years and was a powerful force in bringing the university up to top rank, not only in the South but among other major institutions nationwide. His support was instrumental in the growth of the university into new fields, and he laid the groundwork for the creation of an outstanding library that could offer backing for all aspects of research, teaching, and service to the state.

Dean Wilson lived to be nearly 103.

WINCHELL, CONSTANCE MABEL (1896-1973) was born in Northampton, Massachusetts. She graduated from the University of Michigan in 1918 and received a certificate from the New York Public Library (NYPL) Library School in 1920. At Michigan, she worked as a student assistant in the catalog department. Later, she was employed in the science and engineering departmental libraries. She spent a year as a high school librarian in Duluth, Minnesota. Following her year of study in the NYPL Library School, Miss Winchell became a librarian with the U.S. Merchant Marine Services lighthouse division. She then returned to the University of Michigan, first in the catalog department and then as a reference assistant. Another opportunity presented itself in 1923, when she was appointed head cataloger of the American Library in Paris, where she remained until July 1925. In September of that year, she accepted a position as a reference assistant at the Columbia University Library under Isadore Gilbert Mudge. She received a master's degree from the School of Library Service in 1930, was promoted to assistant reference librarian at Columbia in 1933, and became reference librarian from 1941 to 1962. She retired in 1962.

Miss Winchell is known widely as the author of the seventh and eighth editions of the ALA's *Guide to Reference Books* (1951 and 1967) and its four supplements. The reference services division of the American Library Association awarded Miss Winchell the Isadore Gilbert Mudge Citation in 1960 for distinguished contributions to reference librarianship.

WINDSOR, PHINEAS LAWRENCE (1871-1965) was born in Chenoa, Illinois. He graduated from Northwestern University in 1895 and from the New York State Library School in 1899. He was an asssistant at the New York State Library in 1899 and at the Library of Congress copyright office from 1900 to 1903. From 1903 to 1909, he was librarian of the University of Texas, and he then became librarian of the University of Illinois and director of the Illinois Library School in 1901 until his retirement in 1940. He was vice-president of the American Library Association in 1923-1924 and the second president of the Association of College and Research Libraries in 1939-1940. He served two terms as president of the Association of American Library Schools, in 1921-1922 and 1934-1935, and two terms as president of the Illinois Library Association, in 1913 and 1935. He was president of the American Library Institute from 1940 to 1943. Columbia University conferred an honorary Litt.D. degree upon him in 1939. He died at age ninety-four.

WINSOR, JUSTIN (1831-1897) was born in Boston and studied at Harvard but did not receive his degree until 1853. From 1852 until 1854, he traveled in Europe, studied French and German, and also mastered Dutch, Spanish, Portuguese, and Italian. After returning to Boston in 1854, Winsor contributed prolifically to periodicals until 1868. Late in 1866, he became a trustee of the Boston Public Library, served as active head for a time, and then continued as librarian for nine years. In 1877, he resigned that position to succeed John L. Sibley as librarian of Harvard College. Before assuming his new duties, he went to London to attend the first International Conference of Librarians.

Winsor was one of the founders of the *Library Journal* and of the Americn Library Association. He was the first president of the ALA (1876-1885) and served another term in 1897. As an author and editor, he produced a number of monumental reference works, such as *The Reader's Handbook of the American Revolution* (1879), *The Memorial History of Boston* (4 volumes, 1880-1881), and *Narrative and Critical History of America* (8 volumes, 1886). He had a particular interest in maps and became the leading cartographer in the United States.

WROTH, LAWRENCE COUNSELMAN (1884-1970) was a native of Baltimore and graduated from Johns Hopkins University in 1905. He was often called the dean of American bibliographers, a tribute to his many distinguished publications. He was librarian of the John Carter Brown Library at Brown University from 1923 to 1957 and a consultant on rare books for the Pierpont Morgan Library and the Library of Congress. Earlier in his career, he was librarian of the Maryland Diocesan Library from 1907 to 1912 and then assistant librarian of the Enoch Pratt Free Library in Baltimore. For two years, 1917 to 1919, he was in military service in France during World War I. He also attended classes at the Sorbonne before returning to Baltimore. Wroth was president of the Bibliographical Society of America from 1931 to 1933.

WYER, JAMES INGERSOLL (1869-1955) was born in Red Wing, Minnesota. He and his half-brother, Malcolm G. Wyer, were both destined to achieve distinction in the library world. At age twenty-six, Wyer decided to become a librarian and entered the New York State Library School at Albany in 1896. He had previously gained some experience as an assistant at the Minneapolis Public Library. The Albany school had a distinguished faculty headed by Melvil Dewey. While completing the two-year course, Wyer was employed as an assistant at the New York State Library. After receiving a B.L.S. degree in 1898, Wyer became librarian of the University of Nebraska. From 1899 to 1901, he was president of the Nebraska Library Association, and from 1902 to 1909, he was secretary of the American Library Association. In 1906, he accepted the position of reference librarian at the New York State

Library and of vice-director of the library school. He had been awarded the M.L.S. degree by the school in 1905.

In 1911, a fire destroyed almost all of the state library's collections, and Wyer was confronted with the large task of rebuilding its resources. The library was closed for two years. When it reopened in 1913, Wyer reported 335,000 volumes on the library's shelves. An outstanding program of cooperation was developed with several hundred other libraries around New York state.

Wyer was president of the National Association of State Libraries in 1914. From 1908 until 1926, he served as director of the New York State Library School until it was transferred to Columbia University. Wyer's status as a leading educator was recognized by his election in 1915 as president of the Association of American Library Schools. He was president of the American Library Association in 1910-1911 and president of the New York Library Association in 1913-1914.

Two influential texts written by Wyer were used widely: *U.S. Government Documents: Federal, State and City* (1922) and *Reference Work* (1927).

Wyer retired as director of the New York State Library in 1938 after thirty years in the position — an all-time record.

WYER, MALCOLM GLENN (1877-1965) was born in Concordia, Kansas, and grew up in Minnesota. He earned two degrees from the University of Minnesota, in 1899 and 1901. He next entered the New York State Library School and received the B.L.S. degree in 1903. Steps in his library career included a year as librarian of Colorado College in Colorado Springs. This was followed by his appointment as acting librarian and then director of the State University of Iowa Library, starting in 1904. There he consolidated departmental collections and book budgets, recataloged the entire collection, and hired Harriet E. Howe as cataloger. In 1913, he became librarian of the University of Nebraska, where he remained until 1924, when in his final move he became librarian of the Denver Public Library. At Denver, he took a special interest in developing a strong reference collection, a fine arts department, and an extensive Western history collection. His concern for the Rocky Mountain region was demonstrated when he was a leader in the creation of the Bibliographic Center for Research of the Rocky Mountain Region, an organization for which Wyer served as president from 1942 to 1952. Seeing the need for library education, Wyer also promoted the establishment of the University of Denver School of Librarianship in 1931. By 1933, Wyer was simultaneously librarian of the Denver Public Library, dean of the School of Librarianship, and director of the University of Denver libraries. Harriet Howe was persuaded to come to Denver from the University of Chicago Graduate Library School as director of the school, although Wyer remained deeply involved in the school's operations. In 1935, the Adult Education Center was set up in the Denver Public Library, an idea inspired by Wyer.

Wyer was active in a number of professional organizations, serving at different times as president of the Iowa, Nebraska, and Colorado library associations (1910-1927). He was twice vice-president of the American Library Association, in 1922-1923 and 1928-1929, and president of the ALA for the 1936-1937 term. In recognition of his achievements, he received many honorary degrees and other honors.

YONGE, ENA LAURA (1895-1971) was born in India. Her education was completed at Barnard College, starting in 1917 and continuing until her retirement in 1962. She had a long and noteworthy career at the American Geographical Society in New York City. Under her guidance, the society's holdings became the largest geographical library in the western hemisphere, with a particularly noteworthy map collection. She was closely involved with the activities of geographical organizations such as the Association of American Geographers. She was author of a standard manual for classification and cataloging of maps and a major work, *A Catalogue of Early Globes Made Prior to 1850*. She also found time to act as a tour leader and world traveler.

YOUNG, JOHN RUSSELL (1840-1899), appointed by President William McKinley in 1897 to succeed Spofford, was Irish born. He was a journalist and served as U.S. minister to China. After a long career as a journalist and diplomat, Young was nominated as librarian of Congress by President McKinley in 1897 and was immediately confirmed by the Senate. However, he was in the office only until 1899, when he died. During that time, Spofford was appointed chief assistant librarian. During Young's tenure, a balanced staff was arranged by hiring 10 percent blacks, and one-quarter of the total were women. New divisions of the library were created, and a general reorganization increased the institution's efficiency.

The British Museum's Principal Librarians, Secretaries, and Keepers of Departments

The Principal Librarians
From *Director and Principal Librarian* [1989])

1756 Gowin Knight
1772 Matthew Maty
1776 Charles Morton
1799 Joseph Planta
1827 Henry Ellis
1856 Antonio Panizzi
1866 John Winter Jones
1878 Edward Augustus Bond

1888 Edward Maunde Thompson
1909 Frederic George Kenyon
1931 George Francis Hill
1936 Edgar John Forsdyke
1950 Thomas Downing Kendrick
1958 Frank Chalton Francis
1969 Sir Thomas Wolfenden

The Secretaries
(Since 1787)

1787 Edward Whitaker Gray
1806 Edward Bray
1814 Henry Ellis
1828 The Reverend Josiah Forshall

1926 Arundell James Kennedy Esdaile
1940 John Humphrey Witney
1946 Frank Chalton Francis
1948 Bentley P. C. Bridgewater

The Keepers of Departments of Printed Books, 1756-1966
(from *Principal Keeper* [1945])

1756 Matthew Maty
1765 The Reverend Samuel Harper
1803 The Reverend William Beloe
1806 Henry Ellis
1812 The Reverend Hervey Baber
1837 Antonio Panizzi
1856 John Winter Jones
1866 Thomas Watts
1869 William Brenchley Rye
1875 George Bullen
1890 Richard Garnett

1899 George Knottesford Fortescue
1912 Arthur William Kaye Miller
1914 George Frederick Barwick
1919 Alfred William Pollard
1924 Robert Farquhareson Sharp
1930 Wilfred Alexander Marsden
1943 Henry Thomas
1948 Cecil Bernard Oldman
1959 Robert Andrew Wilson
1966 Arthur Hugh Chaplin

Other national libraries came into existence at various times in Scotland, Wales, Spain, Portugal, Italy, Germany, Austria, Russia, and other European countries and in Canada, Latin America, Japan, and Turkey.

The Library of Congress and Its Librarians

The Library of Congress

The Library of Congress dates back to near the creation of the U.S. Congress. Before moving to the new capital in Washington, the Congress had relied for its book needs upon the New York State Society Library and, in Philadelphia, upon the collections of the Library Company. It was recognized, however, that other provisions would be required in Washington. The transfer bill, signed by John Adams in April 1800, included a section establishing the Library of Congress and appropriating $5,000 for the purchase of books and suitable space for their housing. The view of the joint committee set up to supervise the initial stages was that the library should be a simple, functional collection of working tools. A second law passed by Congress in 1802 called for the appointment of a librarian.

Librarians of Congress

Beckley, John James (1757-1807), the first librarian of Congress, nominated by Thomas Jefferson, served 1802-1807.

Margruder, Patrick (1768-1819), nominated by Thomas Jefferson, served 1807-1815.

Watterson, George (1783-1854), nominated by James Madison, served 1815-1829.

Meehan, John Silva (1793-1867), nominated by Andrew Jackson, served 1829-1867.

Stephenson, John G. (1828-1883), nominated by Abraham Lincoln, served 1861-1864.

Spofford, Ainsworth Rand (1825-1908), nominated by Abraham Lincoln, served 1864-1897.

Young, John Russell (1840-1899), nominated by William McKinley, served 1897-1899.

Putnam, Herbert (1861-1955), nominated by William McKinley, served 1899-1939.

MacLeish, Archibald (1892-1982), nominated by Franklin D. Roosevelt, served 1939-1944.

Evans, Luther (1902-1981), nominated by Harry S. Truman, served 1945-1953.

Mumford, Lawrence Quincy (1903-1982), nominated by Dwight D. Eisenhower, served 1954-1974.

Boorstin, Daniel J. (1914-), nominated by Gerald R. Ford, served 1975-1987.

Billington, James Hadley (1929-), nominated by Ronald Reagan, served 1987-to present.

National Librarians

As identified by Frances Laverne Carroll and Philip J. Schwartz in their *Biographical Directory of National Librarians*, the following were the national librarians of the world in 1989:

Albania, Valdete Sala, Director
Algeria, Mahmoud-Agha Bouayed, Director
Angola, Gabriela Antunes, Director
Argentina, Dardo Cuneo, Director
Aruba, Alice Van Romondt, Director
Australia, Warren Horton, Director General
Austria, Magda Strebl, Director General
Bangladesh, Mahbubul Karim, Director
Belgium, Martin Wittek, Director
Belize, Lawrence Vernon, Chief Librarian
Benin, Noel Amoussou, Director
Bhutan, Lopen Pemala, Director
Bolivia, Gunnar Mendoza, Director
Botswana, Basiamang Garebakwena, Director
Brazil, Maria Alice Barroso, Director General
Bulgaria, Peter Karaangov, Director
Canada, Georges Cartier, Director General
Chile, Campus Menendez, Envique, Director
China, Peoples Republic, Ren Jiyu, Director
China, Republic, Chen-Ku Wang, Director
Colombia, Conrado Zuluaga, Director
Cuba, Julio Leriverend Brusone, Director
Czechoslovakia, V. Mrusnoviz, Director
Denmark, Erland Volding Nielson, Librarian
Dominican Republic, Roberto De Soto, Director
Ecuador, Ricardo Descalzi, Director
Egypt, Sa ád Rashid, Director
El Salvador, Jose Astul Yanes, Director
Ethiopia, Arefaine Belay, Department Head
Finland, Esko Hakli, Director General
France, LeRoy Ladurie Emmanuel, Administrator
Gambia, Sally P. C. Njie, Chief Librarian
German Democratic Republic, Helmut Rotzsch, Director General
Germany, Federal Republic, Franz Georg Kaltwasser, Director
Ghana, Christina Kwei, Deputy Director
Greece, Panayolis Niccolopoulos, Director

Greenland, Keld Lund, Director
Guatemala, Flory de Borja, Director
Guyana, Joan Christiana, Director
Haiti, Denise J. Savain, Director
Honduras, Miguel Angel Garcia, Director
Hungary, Gyula Juhasz, Director General
Iceland, Finnbogi Gudmunsson, National Librarian
India, Ashin Das Gupta, Director
Indonesia, Mastini Hardjoprakoso, National Librarian
Iran, Hassan Shahrestani, Director
Iraq, Abdul Hameed Alwaehi, Director
Ireland, Michael Hewson, Director
Israel, Malachi Beit-Arie, Director
Italy, Anna Maria Vichi Giorgetti, Director
Jamaica, Stephney Ferguson, Director
Japan, Kiyohide Ibusuki, Librarian
Jordan, Ahmad Sharkas, Director
Kenya, A. R. Oluoch, Director
Korea, Republic, Soon-Ho Choo, Chief Librarian
Lebanon, Abdallah Tabbah, Director
Luxembourg, Jul Christophory, Director
Malaysia, Donald E. K. Whasuriya, Director General
Mali, Abdoul Aziz Diallo, Director
Malta, John B. Sultana, Librarian
Mauritius, B. Q. Goordyal, Librarian
Mexico, Jesus Marquez Narvaez, General Coordinator
Monaco, Herve Baral, Conservator
Nepal, Sharma Subedi Madhusudan, Chairman
Netherlands, Jarob Van Heijst, Librarian
New Zealand, Peter Scott, National Librarian
Nicaragua, Carlos A. Bravo, Director
Nigeria, Mu Ázu H. Wali, Director
Norway, Bendik Rugaas, Director
Pakistan, Abdul Hafeez Akhtar, Director
Panama, Algis Borrero, Director
Paraguay, H. Sanchez Quell, Director
Peru, Juan Mejica Baca, Director
Philippines, Serafin Quiason, Director
Poland, Stanislaw Czajka, Director
Portugal, Manuel V. Cabral, Director
Rumania, Angela Popescu-Bradiceni, Director
Scotland, Edward Frederick Denis Roberts, Librarian

Sierra Leone, Gloria Dillsworth, Chief Librarian
Singapore, Hedwig Anuar, Director
Somalia, Hassan Noor Farah, Director
South Africa, Itans Aschenborn, Director
Spain, Manuel Mundo, Director
Sri Lanka, Srimathie Desoya, Librarian
Swaziland, Benjamin Kingsley, Director
Sweden, Lars Tynell, National Librarian
Switzerland, Franz Georg Maier, Director
Syria, Ghassan Lah ham, Director General
Tanzania, Ezekiel E. Kaungamno, Director
Thailand, Kullasae Germankip, Director
Tunisia, Raruf Belhassey, Director
USSR, N. S. Kartasov, Director
United Kingdom, British Library, Kenneth Cooper, Chief Executive
    Peter Lewis, Director General
United States, James H. Billington, Librarian of Congress
U.S. National Agricultural Library, Joseph Howard, Director
U.S. National Library of Medicine, Donald Lindberg, Director
Uruguay, Enrique Fierro, Director
Vatican City, Leonard Boyle, Prefect
Venezuela, Virginia Betancourt, Director
Wales, Brynley Roberts, Librarian
Yugoslavia, Dusan Martinovic, Director
Zaire, Zere Makangila, Director
Zimbabwe, Robin William Doust, Librarian

Appendix D

Notable Foreign Librarians

Japan

Legislation to establish the National Diet Library was drafted by Charles H. Brown of Iowa State University and Verner W. Clapp of the Library of Congress on a mission to Japan in 1947. The following year, Robert Downs of the University of Illinois went to Tokyo to advise on the library's organization. The first chief librarian was Dr. Tokujiro Kanamori. His successors were Masahiro Arao, Minoru Kishida, and Kiyohide Ibusuk. Other leaders in the library profession in Japan were Takeo Urata, director of the Tokyo University Library, and Yoshinari Tsuda, librarian of the Keio Medical College Library.

Turkey

After establishment of the Turkish National Library in 1948, its first director was Adnan Oturen. Other prominent figures were Furvzen Olşen, director of the Middle East Technical University Library in Ankara, and Osman Ersoy, the first director of the University of Ankara Library School.

Australia

The modern library movement in Australia is greatly indebted to two leaders: Andrew Osborn, former director of the University of Sydney Library, and Harrison Bryan, director of the University of Sydney Library and subsequently director of the National Library of Australia. Also influential was Jean Hagger, head of the department of librarianship at the Royal Melbourne Institute of Technology.

Egypt

Mohammed El-Hadi has had a distinguished career as an information science specialist serving in Egypt, Morocco, and Saudi Arabia.

Pakistan

Abdul Moid has served as a university librarian and library school director in Pakistan and Nigeria.

South America

Librarianship in South America was influenced by Luís Floren, late director of the Inter-American Library School.

South Africa

Another prominent library educator is Rhoda Barry, a South African librarian.

Philippines

Also in the field of education is Ursula Picache, on the faculty of the Philippines Institute of Library Science.

Robert Vosper, from the University of California at Los Angeles, has participated actively in the International Federation of Library Associations. His personal observations were published in *International Library Horizons* (Washington, D.C.: Library of Congress, 1989), in which he identifies a number of distinguished foreign librarians:

> Herman Liebaers, former royal librarian of Belgium
> Jorge Aguayo, librarian, University of Havana
> Harold Tveteras, Norway
> Preben Kirkagard, Denmark
> Margreet Wijnstroom, Holland
> Gosta Otternik, Sweden
> Joachim Wieder, Germany
> Rudolf Malek, Czechoslovakia
> Esko Hahli, Finland
> N. M. Sikorsky, Lenin State Library
> Joyce Robinson, Jamaica
> Joseph Soosai, Malay States

Presidents of the American Library Association

Many of the leading librarians of the United States and Canada became presidents of the American Library Association. A complete list of these individuals follows. They represent various fields — public, college, university, and special libraries and library education — since the founding of the association in 1876:

Presidents	Terms of Office
Justin Winsor (died October 22, 1897)	1876-1885
William Frederick Poole (died March 1, 1894)	1885-1887
Charles Ammi Cutter (died September 8, 1903)	1887-1889
Frederick Morgan Crunden (died October 28, 1911)	1889-1890
Melvil Dewey (died December 26, 1931)	1890-July 1891
Samuel Swett Green (died December 8, 1918)	July-November 1891
William Isaac Fletcher (died June 6, 1917)	1891-1892
Melvil Dewey (died December 26, 1931)	1892-1893
Josephus Nelson Larned (died August 15, 1913)	1893-1894
Henry Munson Utley (died February 16, 1917)	1894-1895
John Cotton Dana (died July 21, 1929)	1895-1896
William Howard Brett (died August 24, 1918)	1896-1897
Justin Winsor (died October 22, 1897)	July-October 1897
Herbert Putnam (died August 14, 1955)	January-August 1898
William Coolidge Lane (died March 18, 1931)	1898-1899
Reuben Gold Thwaites (died October 22, 1913)	1899-1900
Henry James Carr (died Mary 21, 1929)	1900-1901
John Shaw Billings (died March 11, 1913)	1901-1902
James Kendall Hosmer (died May 18, 1927)	1902-1903
Herbert Putnam (died August 14, 1955)	1903-1904
Ernest Cushing Richardson (died June 3, 1939)	1904-1905
Frank Pierce Hill (died August 28, 1941)	1905-1906
Clement Walker Andrews (died November 20, 1930)	1906-1907
Arthur Elmore Bostwick (died February 13, 1942)	1907-1908
Charles Henry Gould (died July 30, 1919)	1908-1909
Nathaniel D. C. Hodges (died November 25, 1927)	1909-1910
James Ingersoll Wyer (died November 1, 1955)	1910-1911
Theresa West Elmendorf (died September 4, 1932)	1911-1912
Henry Eduard Legler (died September 13, 1917)	1912-1913
Edwin Hatfield Anderson (died April 29, 1947)	1913-1914
Hiller Crowell Wellman (died February 3, 1956)	1914-1915

Mary Wright Plummer (died September 21, 1916)	1915-1916
Walter Lewis Brown (died October 16, 1931)	1916-1917
Thomas Lynch Montgomery (died October 1, 1929)	1917-1918
William Warner Bishop (died February 19, 1955)	1918-1919
Chalmers Hadley (died May 11, 1958)	1919-1920
Alice S. Tyler (died April 18, 1944)	1920-1021
Azariah Smith Root (died October 2, 1927)	1921-1922
George Burwell Utley (died October 4, 1946)	1922-1923
Judson Toll Jennings (died February 8, 1948)	1923-1924
Herman H. B. Meyer (died January 16, 1937)	1924-1925
Charles F. D. Belden (died October 23, 1931)	1925-1926
George H. Locke (died January 28, 1937)	1926-1927
Carl B. Roden (died October 25, 1956)	1927-1928
Linda A. Eastman (died April 5, 1963)	1928-1929
Andrew Keogh (died February 14, 1953)	1929-1930
Adam Strohm (died October 30, 1951)	1930-1931
Josephine Admas Rathbone (died May 17, 1941)	1931-1932
Harry Miller Lyndenberg (died April 16, 1960)	1932-1933
Gratia A. Countryman (died July 26, 1953)	1933-1934
Charles H. Compton (died March 17, 1966)	1934-1935
Louis Round Wilson (died December 9, 1979)	1935-1936
Malcolm Glenn Wyer (died December 31, 1965)	1936-1937
Harrison Warwick Craver (died July 26, 1951)	1937-1938
Milton James Ferguson (died October 23, 1954)	1938-1939
Ralph Munn (died January 22, 1975)	1939-1940
Essae Martha Culver (died January 2, 1973)	1940-1941
Charles Harvey Brown (died January 19, 1960)	1941-1942
Keyes D. Meltcalf (died November 3, 1983)	1942-1943
Althea H. Warren (died December 21, 1958)	1943-1944
Carl Vitz (died January 28, 1981)	1944-1945
Ralph A. Ulveling (died March 21, 1980)	1945-1946
Mary U. Rothrock (died January 30, 1976)	1946-1947
Paul North Rice (died April 16, 1967)	1947-1948
Errett Weir McDiarmid	1948-1949
Milton E. Lord (died February 1985)	1949-1950
Clarence R. Graham	1950-1951
Loleta Dawson Fyan	1951-1952
Robert Bingham Downs	1952-1953
Flora Belle Ludington (died March 23, 1967)	1953-1954
L. Quincy Mumford (died August 15, 1982)	1954-1955
John S. Richards (died December 1979)	1955-1956
Ralph R. Shaw (died October 17, 1972)	1956-1957
Lucile Morsch (died July 3, 1972)	1957-1958

Emerson Greenaway	1958-1959
Benjamin E. Powell (died March 11, 1981)	1959-1960
Frances Lander Spain	1960-1961
Florrinell F. Morton	1961-1962
James E. Bryan	1962-1963
Frederick H. Wagman	1963-1964
Edwin Castagna (died November 26, 1983)	1964-1965
Robert Vosper	1965-1966
Mary V. Gaver	1966-1967
Foster E. Mohrhardt	1967-1968
Roger McDonough	1968-1969
William S. Dix (died February 22, 1978)	1969-1970
Lillian M. Bradshaw	1970-1971
Keith Doms	1971-1972
Katharine Laich	1972-1973
Jean E. Lowrie	1973-1974
Edward G. Holley	1974-1975
Allie Beth Martin (died April 11, 1976)	1975-April 1976
Clara Stanton Jones (acting president)	April 11-July 22, 1976
Clara Stanton Jones	July 1976-1977
Eric Moon	1977-1978
Russell Shank	1978-1979
Thomas J. Galvin	1979-1980
Peggy A. Sullivan	1980-1981
Elizabeth W. (Betty) Stone	1981-1982
Carol A. Nemeyer	1982-1983
Brooke E. Sheldon	1983-1984
E. J. Josey	1984-1985
Beverly P. Lynch	1985-1986
Regina Minudri	1986-1987
Margaret E. Chisholm	1987-1988
F. William Summers	1988-1989
Patricia Berger	1989-1990
Richard M. Dougherty	1990-1991

Executive Secretaries of the American Library Association
(Later Called Executive Directors)

Executive Secretaries	Terms of Office
Melvil Dewey	1879-1890
William E. Parker and Mary Salome Cutler	1890-July 1891
Frank Pierce Hill	1891-1895
Henry Livingston Elmendorf	1895-1896
Rutherford Platt Hayes	1896-1897
Melvil Dewey	1897-1898
Henry James Carr	1898-1900
Frederick Winthrop Faxon	1900-1902
James Ingersoll Wyer	1902-1909
(Edward C. Hovey, executive officer, 1902-1909)	
Chalmers Hadley	1901-1911
George Burwell Utley	1911-April 1920
Carl H. Milan	1920-1948
Harold F. Brigham (interim)	July-August 1948
John MacKenzie Cory	1948-1951
David H. Clift	1951-1958
David H. Clift (emeritus; died October 12, 1973)	1958-August 1972
Robert Wedgeworth	August 1972-1985
Thomas Galvin	December 1985-1989
Linda F. Crismond	1989 to present

Treasurers of the American Library Association 1876-1990

Treasurers	Terms of Office
Melvil Dewey	1876-1877
Charles Evans	1877-1878
Melvil Dewey	1878-1879
Frederick Jackson	1879-1880
Melvil Dewey	1880-1881
Frederick Jackson	1881-1882
James Lyman Whitney	1882-1886
Henry James Carr	1886-1893
George Watson Cole	1893-1895
Edwin Hatfield Anderson	1895-1896
George Watson Cole	1896 (September-November)
Charles Knowles Bolton	1896-1897
Gardner Maynard Jones	1897-1906
George Franklin Bowerman	1906-1907
Anderson Hoyt Hopkins	1907-1908
Purd B. Wright	1908-1910
Carl B. Roden	1910-1920
Edward D. Tweedel	1920-1927
Matthew S. Dudgeon	1927-1941
Rudolph H. Gjelsness	1941-1947
Harold F. Brigham	1947-1949
R. Russell Munn	1949-1952
Raymond C. Lindquist	1952-1956
Richard B. Sealock	1956-1960
Arthur Yabroff	1960-1964
Ralph Blasingame	1964-1968
Robert B. McClarren	1968-1972
Frank B. Sessa	1972-1976
William Chait	1976-1980
Herbert Biblo	1980-1984
Patricia Glass Schuman	1984-1988
Carla J. Stoffle	1988 to present

Presidents and Executive Directors of the Association of College and Research Libraries

Another group, principally college and university librarians, has served as presidents of the Association of College and Research Libraries since the ACRL was established in 1938. A complete list follows:

Presidents	Term of Office
Frank K. Walter	1838-1939
Phineas L. Windsor	1939-1940
Robert B. Downs	1940-1941
Donald Coney	1941-1942
Mabel L. Conat	1942-1943
Charles B. Shaw	1943-1944
Winifred Ver Nooy	1944-1945
Blanche Prichard McCrum	1945-1946
Errett Weir McDiarmid	1946-1947
William H. Carlson	1947-1948
Benjamin E. Powell	1948-1949
Wyllis E. Wright	1949-1950
Charles M. Adams	1950-1951
Ralph E. Ellsworth	1951-1952
Robert W. Severance	1952-1953
Harriett D. MacPherson	1953-1954
Guy R. Lyle	1954-1955
Robert Vosper	1955-1956
Robert W. Orr	1956-1957
Eileen Thornton	1957-1958
Lewis C. Branscomb	1958-1959
Wyman W. Parker	1959-1960
Edmon Low	1960-1961
Ralph E. Ellsworth	1961-1962
Katherine M. Stokes	1962-1963
Neal R. Harlow	1963-1964
Archie L. McNeal	1964-1965
Helen Margaret Brown	1965-1966
Ralph E. McCoy	1966-1967
James Humphrey III	1967-1968
David Kaser	1968-1969
Philip J. McNiff	1969-1970
Anne C. Edmonds	1970-1971

Joseph Reason	1971-1972
Russell Shank	1972-1973
Norman E. Tanis	1973-1974
H. William Axford	1974-1975
Louise Giles	1975-1976
Connie R. Dunlap	1976-1977
Eldred R. Smith	1977-1978
Evan I. Farber	1978-1979
LeMoyne W. Anderson	1979-1980
Millicent D. Abell	1980-1981
David C. Weber	1981-1982
Carla J. Stoffle	1982-1983
Joyce Ball	1983-1984
Sharon J. Rogers	1984-1985
Sharon Anne Hogan	1985-1986
Hannelore Rader	1986-1987
Joanne Euster	1987-1988
Joseph A. Boisse	1988-1989

Executive Directors

N. Orwin Rush	1947-1949
Arthur T. Hamlin	1949-1956
Richard B. Harwell	1957-1961
Mark M. Gormley	1961-1962
Joseph H. Reason	1962-1963
George M. Bailey	1963-1968
J. Donald Thomas	1968-1972
Beverly P. Lynch	1977-1984
Julie A. C. Virgo	1977-1984
JoAn S. Segal	1984 to present

American Library Pioneers

A further effort was made to single out the early library leaders in a series of biographies, "The American Library Pioneers Series," published by the American Library Association. It was originally edited by Arthur C. Bostwick. The seven published volumes were as follows: *John Shaw Billings,* by H. M. Lydenberg; *Samuel Swett Green,* by R. K. Shaw; *Charles Ammi Cutter,* by W. P. Cutter; *William Howard Brett,* by Linda A. Eastman; *John Cotton Dana,* by Charles Hadley; *Melvil Dewey,* by Fremont Rider; and *Charles Coffin Jewett,* by Joseph A. Barrone.

An eighth volume in the series, edited by Emily Miller Danton, was entitled *Pioneering Leaders in Librarianship* (Chicago: ALA, 1953). It included eighteen biographies by various authors of the following individuals: Clement Walker Andrews, Sarah B. Askew, Arthur E. Bostwick, Richard Rogers Bowker, Miriam E. Carey, Jennie M. Flexner, James L. Gillis, J. C. M. Hanson, Caroline Maria Harris, Joseph Nelson Larned, Henry Eduard Legler, Eunice Rockwood Oberly, Ernest Cushing Richardson, Minerva Sanders, Katharine Sharp, Elizabeth Sohier, Mary L. Titcomb, and Alice Sarah Tyler.

Forty Leaders of the Library Movement

For the seventy-fifty anniversary, in 1951, of the founding of the American Library Association, the ALA library history round table, under the chairmanship of Wayne Shirley, dean of Pratt Institute's library school, undertook to name forty leaders of the library movement since 1876, The results were published in the *Library Journal* on March 15, 1951, in the following article:

A LIBRARY HALL OF FAME
For the 75th Anniversary

The *Library Journal,* in this issue, is taking a backward look over the past 75 years of library history as a prelude to joining in the American Library Association's Anniversary emphasis on "The Heritage of the U.S.A. in Times of Crisis."

Seventy-five years is not a long span. At the great 50th Anniversary Convention in Philadelphia, two of A.L.A.'s founders, Mr. Dewey and Mr. Bowker, were the speakers. As with all chronicles, whether of nations or of groups, the values are best appreciated by recalling the individuals who gave direction and color to the record.

To bring the names of the leaders forward as pleasant memories to many, and as inspiration to the leaders of the next quarter century, *Library Journal* has ventured to make a list of the names of outstanding librarians of the past with a brief paragraph placing these men and women in the library world while suggesting the character of their special contributions.

That this list of names should be as nearly acceptable to all as possible, the *Journal*, after canvassing past library records, made a tentative list. This tenative list was sent to 20 librarians known to be familiar with and interested in library history. These 20 were asked to cross off and add to the list. These replies, with their very helpful comments, provided a vote by which to decide on the inclusions.

As further aid to the right listings, the A.L.A., at Midwinter meetings, asked its History Round Table to represent them, and Wayne Shirley, dean of the library school at Pratt Institute accepted the responsibility.

It has been agreed that this present list should not include the living, however obvious and significant had been their contribution. The list, with such additions, would promptly be doubled.

It was further understood that only librarians should be included, though the publishers of *Library Journal* have not failed to be pleased that there have been so many suggestions that the name of R. R. Bowker belonged on any such list.

Mary Eileen Ahern	1865-1938
Edwin H. Anderson	1861-1947
Sarah B. Askew	1863-1942
John Shaw Billings	1839-1913
Sarah C. N. Bogle	1870-1932
Arthur E. Bostwick	1860-1942
William Howard Brett	1846-1918
Frederick M. Crunden	1847-1911
Charles A. Cutter	1837-1903
John Cotton Dana	1856-1929
Melvil Dewey	1851-1931
Wilberforce Eames	1855-1937
Theresa Elmendorf	1955-1932
Charles Evans	1950-1935
Salome C. Fairchild	1865-1921
William I. Fletcher	1844-1917
Jennie Flexner	1882-1944
William E. Foster	1851-1930
James L. Gillis	1857-1917
Samuel Swett Green	1837-1918
J. C. M. Hanson	1864-1943
Mary E. Hazeltine	1868-1949
Caroline M. Hewins	1946-1923
Judson T. Jennings	1872-1948
Charles C. Jewett	1816-1868
William C. Lane	1859-1931
Joseph N. Larned	1836-1913
George H. Locke	1870-1937
Charles Martel	1860-1945
Mary W. Plummer	1856-1916
William F. Poole	1821-1894
Josephine Rathbone	1864-1941
Ernest C. Richardson	1860-1939
Ainsworth Spofford	1825-1908
Reuben G. Thwailes	1853-1913
Alice Sarah Tyler	1859-1944
George B. Utley	1876-1948
Justin Winsor	1831-1897

Twenty-five years later, two librarians, William E. Studwell and Byron P. Anderson, offered a similar proposal in an article in *American Libraries* (March 1990), "Why Not a Library Hall of Fame?" Their tentative nominations were the following: Hugh Atkinson, Henriette D. Avram, Verner W. Clapp, Benjamin A. Custer, Charles Ammi Cutter, John Corton Dana, Melvil Dewey, Robert B. Downs, Charles Evans, Charles Coffin Jewett, Margaret Mann, William Frederick Poole, Minnie E. Sears, William J. Well, and H. S. Wilson.

Leaders in American Academic Librarianship

Beta Phi Mu, the library honorary society, undertook to identify *Leaders in American Academic Librarianship* (1925-1975). A book by that title, edited by Wayne A. Wiegand, was published by the ALA in 1983. It included biographies of the following individuals: *Charles Harvey Brown,* by Edward G. Holley; *William S. Dix,* by Michael H. Harris and Mary Ann Tourjee; *Robert B. Downs,* by Arthur P. Young; *Ralph E. Ellsworth,* by Edward R. Johnson; *Lillian Baker Griggs,* by Betty Young; *Guy R. Lyle,* by Philip Dare; *Stephen McCarthy,* by Donald E. Oehlerts; *Blanche P. McCrum,* by Betty Ruth Kondayan; *Keyes DeWitt Metcalf,* by Peter Hernon; *Jerrold Orne,* by Rosemary Ruhig DuMont; *Lawrence Clark Powell,* by Wayne A. Wiegand; *Ralph Shaw,* by I. Bruce Turner; *Maurice R. Tauber,* by Kurt S. Maier; *Robert G. Vosper,* by Betty Milum; and *Louis Round Wilson,* by John Richardson, Jr.

Honorary Members of the American Library Association

Aiken, The Hon. George*
Allain, Alex P.
Asheim, Lester E.
Austin, Edwin C.*
Baker, Augusta
Barnard, Henry*
Bishop, William Warner*
Bowker, Richard Rogers*
Brademas, John
Brown, Charles Harvey*
Carnegie, Andrew*
Carson, Johnny
Chancellor, John Miller*
Chapman, Theodore S.*
Cheney, Frances Neel
Clapp, Verner Warren*
Clements, William L.*
Clift, David H.*
Cole, Fred C.*
Collins, Ross*
Coolidge, Elizabeth Sprague*
Dalton, Jack
Dix, William S.*
Douglas, The Hon. William O.*
Downs, Robet B.
Eames, Wilberforce*
Eastman, Linda A.*
Eliot, Charles William*
Elliot, The Hon. Carl*
Ellsworth, Ralph E.
Evans, Charles*
Evans, Luther H.*
Finley, John H.*
Fiske, Willard*
Fogarty, The Hon. John E.*
Ford, The Hon. William
Francis, Sir Frank
Gaver, Mary V.
Gilman, Daniel Coit*

Grant, Edwin H.*
Grant, S. Hastings*
Guild, Reuben Aldridge*
Haines, Helen E.*
Hale, Edward Everett*
Harris, Ezekiel A.*
Haviland, Virginia
Hill, Frank Pierce*
Hill, The Hon. Lister*
Hoover, Herbert Clark*
Javits, The Hon. Jacob*
Jencks, Charles W.*
Joeckel, Carleton B.*
Jones, Clara Stanton
Jones, Virginia Lacy*
Keppel, Frederick P.*
Kilgour, Frederick
Krettek, Germaine
Lester, Robert MacDonald*
Liebaers, Herman
Low, Edmon*
Lydenberg, Harry Miller*
Martin, Allie Beth* (Special Centennial
   Honorary Membership)
Martin, Lowell A.
Melcher, Daniel*
Melcher, Frederick G.*
Metcalf, Keyes DeWitt*
Milam, Carl Hastings*
Moon, Eric
Moore, Bessie B.
Morton, Elizabeth Homer*
Nelson, Charles Alexander*
Owens, The Hon. Major
Pell, The Hon. Claiborne
Perkins, The Hon. Carl*
Powell, Lawrence Clark
Prince, Frederick O.*
Putnam, Herbert*

* Deceased

Rollins, Charlamae*
Rothrock, Mary U.*
Ruffner, Frederick Gale, Jr.
Shaw, Ralph R.*
Shaw, Spencer G.
Shera, Jesse H.*
Stevens, David H.
Stone, Elizabeth W.
Updike, Daniel Berkeley*
Upson, Anson Judd*
Vanderlip, Frank A.*
Vincent, Bioshop John H.*
Wheeler, Joseph Lewis*
Wilson, Halsey William*
Wilson, Louis Round*
Yound, Virginia G.

* Deceased

Additional Sources of Infomation

Three especially useful sources are:

Dictionary of American Library Biography. Littleton, Colo.: Libraries Unlimited, 1978.

Engelbarts, Rudolf. *Librarian Authors: A Bibliography.* Jefferson, N.C.: McFarland, 1981.

Directory of Library and Information Professionals. Chicago: ALA, 1988.

Other valuable references are:

A.L.A. World Encyclopedia of Library and Information Services. Chicago: ALA, 1980, 1986.

A Biographical Directory of Librarians in the United States and Canada. Chicago: ALA, 1970.

Carroll, Frances Laverne, and Schwartz, Philip J. *Biographical Directory of National Librarians.* London: Mansell, 1989. 134p.

Current Biography. New York: H. W. Wilson, 1940 to date.

Danton, Emily. *Pioneering Leaders in Librarianship.* Chicago: ALA, 1953.

Dictionary of American Biography. New York: Scribner, 1928-1981.

Dictionary of National Biography. London: Smith, Elder, 1908-71.

Dunlap, Leslie W. *Readings in Library History.* New York: Bowker, 1972.

Esdaile, Arundell. *The British Museum Library; a Short History.* London: Allen & Unwin, 1946.

Fenster, Valmai Kirkham. *Out of the State: Notable Wisconsin Women Librarians.* Madison: Wisconsin Women Library Workers, 1985.

Goodrun, Charles A. *The Library of Congress.* New York: Praeger, 1974.

Goodrun, Gene. *The Library of Congress.* New York: Crown, 1987.

Hessel, Alfred. *A History of Libraries.* New Brunswick, N.J.: Scarecrow Press, 1955.

Johnson, Elmer D., and Harris, Michael H. *Histories of Libraries in the Western Worrld.* Metuchen, N.J.: Scarecrow Press, 1976.

Lundy, Kathryn R. *Women View Librarianship: Nine Perspectives.* Chicago: ALA, 1980.

Marshall, John David. *An American Libary History Reader.* Hamden, Conn.: Shoe String Press, 1961.

Thompson, James Westfall. *Ancient Libraries.* Berkeley: Univ. of California Press, 1940.

Thompson, James Westfall. *The Medieval Library.* New York: Hafner, 1957.

Who's Who in America. Chicago: AN. Marquis, 1988-89.

Who Was Who. Chicago: AN. Marquis, 1963-1985.

Who's Who in Library and Information Services, ed. by Joel M. Lee. Chicago: ALA, 1982.

Wiegand, Wayne A. *Leaders in American Academic Librarianship, 1925-1975.* Chicago: ALA, 1983.

Contemporary Authors. Detroit: Gale, 1962 to date.

National Cyclopedia of American Biography. New York: White, 1898 to date.